VOLUNTEER
MANAGEMENT
for Animal Care Organizations

Betsy McFarland

THE **HUMANE** SOCIETY
OF THE UNITED STATES

HUMANE SOCIETY
UNIVERSITY

Betsy McFarland is director of communications
for the Companion Animals section of The
Humane Society of the United States (HSUS).
She speaks regularly at conferences, both
domestically and internationally, on shelter
volunteer management. She holds a degree
in psychology from George Mason University
and a certificate in nonprofit business and
management from the Johns Hopkins
University. She is a member of the Association
for Volunteer Administration.

Second edition
ISBN 0-9748400-1-7
Library of Congress Cataloging-in Publication Data

McFarland, Betsy.
    Volunteer management for animal care organizations/by Betsy McFarland.–
2nd ed.
        p. cm.
    ISBN 0-9748400-1-7
    1. Animal shelters–United States–Personnel management. 2.
Volunteers–United States–Management. I. Humane Society of the United
States. II. Title.
    HV4764.M25 2004
    636.08'32'0683–dc22

                                        2004027130

Printed in the United States of America

Humane Society Press
An affiliate of The Humane Society of the United States
2100 L Street, NW
Washington, D.C. 20037

Acknowledgments

This project was made possible through a generous grant from the Munder Family Foundation. Lee Munder envisioned a hands-on manual that incorporated practical volunteer management tools supported by solid research on volunteerism. The Humane Society of the United States (HSUS) is proud to fulfill his vision, and we thank him for his generous support and thoughtful leadership throughout this project.

Many shelter volunteer managers lent their time and expertise to this project. My sincere thanks go to the following reviewers: Joyce Barton, Potter League for Animals (Middletown, R.I.); Judy Brown, Capital Area Humane Society (Lansing, Mich.); Maggie Huff, Humane Society of Rochester and Monroe County at Lollypop Farm (Fairport, N.Y.); Champaign County Humane Society (Urbana, Ill.); Tamara Kreigh, Fort Wayne Animal Care and Control (Fort Wayne, Ind.); Jodi Schulz, Dumb Friends League (Denver, Colo.); Christine Titus, Seattle Animal Shelter (Seattle, Wash.); and Tree House Animal Foundation (Chicago, Ill.). Numerous shelter staff members and volunteers patiently and thoroughly provided answers to my many questions. A huge thanks goes to every single one of them—there are too many to mention by name, but you know who you are! Additionally, I'd like to thank Betty Stallings for lending to this project her expert advice on the volunteer management field.

Numerous shelters provided sample forms for us to reprint. These include the Arizona Humane Society (Phoenix, Ariz.); Capital Area Humane Society; Champaign County Humane Society; Dumb Friends League; Erie County SPCA (Tonawanda, N.Y.); Fort Wayne Animal Care and Control; Hawaiian Humane Society (Honolulu, Hawaii); the Humane Society of Rochester and Monroe County at Lollypop Farm; Iowa City/Coralville Animal Care and Adoption Center (Iowa City, Iowa); Larimer Humane Society (Ft. Collins, Colo.); Monadnock Humane Society (West Swanzey, N.H.); Montgomery Humane Society (Montgomery, Ala.); the Potter League for Animals; Seattle Animal Shelter; and Wayside Waifs (Kansas City, Mo.).

This manual would not have been possible without the contributions of my colleagues at The HSUS. Many thanks go to Carrie Allan, Martha Armstrong, Traci Bryant, Bill DeRosa, Geoff Handy, Nancy Lawson, Kate Pullen, Bob Roop, Andrew Rowan, Valerie Sheppard, and John Snyder. Special thanks go to Kathleen Allspaw at Tufts University for assisting with the academic research and to Julie Miller-Dowling for editing the manuscript.

Cover Photography by: Ellen Kamilakis/FCPD Animal Services Division, Potter League for Animals, and Tom McManus/Seattle Animal Shelter

Contents

HSUS Volunteer Management Survey Results

The HSUS conducted an online survey of 289 animal-shelter-volunteer managers during November and December 2002. This is the first national volunteer management survey conducted for the sheltering field (see Appendix).

While the survey is not a representative sample, the results were interesting and confirmed what we've suspected all along: many shelters haven't taken the time to plan properly and ensure that the necessary management tools are in place to manage their volunteers successfully.

Here is a summary of some of the findings:

■ Most of the organizations responding to the survey handle five thousand animals or fewer annually.

Table 1

Number of Animals Handled per Year

Animals Handled per Year	Number of Respondents	Percent of Respondents
Less than 2,500	122	57
2,501–5,000	27	12.6
5,001–10,000	35	16.4
10,001+	30	14

■ Most respondents—44 percent—work for a private humane organization, 28 percent work for a municipal animal control agency, and the remaining 28 percent work with a private organization that has a contract to provide housing or animal control services. These demographics are consistent with previous HSUS surveys.

■ Results indicate that most shelters are not taking full advantage of management tools that would greatly help them improve their volunteer programs.

Table 2

Management Tools

Tool	Percent of Respondents Using the Tool
Interviews or Orientations	73
Liability Waivers	69
Applications	66
Job Descriptions	50
Schedules	50
Formal Training	46
Volunteer Manuals	42
Contracts	22
Performance Reviews	7

- Only 8 percent of respondents have a full-time paid volunteer coordinator. Shelters with dedicated full-time coordinators tend to handle larger numbers of animals (five thousand or more per year).

- Nearly 80 percent of respondents say that staff view volunteers as very or somewhat helpful. Specifically, volunteers are considered to be very helpful in shelters where they receive training.

Table 3

Staff Perception of Volunteers

Staff Feels Volunteers Are:		Formal Training Run by Paid Staff Using Written Materials	No Formal Training— Volunteers Shadow Staff	Current Volunteers Train New Volunteers	No Formal Training Program
Very Helpful	Number	37	30	29	19
	Percent	51.4	44.1	70.7	38.8
Somewhat Helpful	Number	31	28	7	14
	Percent	43.1	41.2	17.1	28.6
No Opinion	Number	1		4	6
	Percent	1.4		9.8	12.2
Okay, but Not That Helpful	Number	2	9	1	7
	Percent	2.8	13.2	2.4	14.3
Disruptive to Daily Work	Number	1	1		3
	Percent	1.4	1.5		6.1
TOTAL	Number	72	68	41	49
	Percent	100	100	100	100

- Of the 253 respondents who answered the question about boards of directors, only 42 percent feel their board members are either very helpful or at least somewhat helpful in day-to-day activities.

- When it comes to recruiting volunteers, 63 percent advertise for volunteers on their web sites, 54 percent advertise in their newsletters, and 45 percent advertise in the community newspaper.

- Some of the most common jobs volunteers perform for shelters include:
  - Socialize/walk dogs (82 percent)
  - Socialize cats (80 percent)

- Special events (78 percent)
- Foster care (70 percent)
- Kennel and cage cleaning (69 percent)
- Fund-raising (67 percent)

■ Relatively little formal training is available for shelter staff members to learn how to work with and manage volunteers. The majority (44 percent) learn on the job, while 23 percent are given in-house training. Few respondents (only 4.8 percent) report sending staff to off-site training in volunteer management.

■ Sixty percent of respondents say they provide written standard operating procedures to staff.

■ Eighty-two percent say "Thank you" to their volunteers, while only 66 percent report saying, "Thank you" to staff. About half of respondents (49 percent) hold recognition events for volunteers, but only 27 percent hold recognition events for staff.

■ Approximately 50 percent of volunteer applicants actually become volunteers. (This suggests that follow-up after the orientation or application process may be a problem.)

■ Forty-four and a half percent of respondents indicate they actively seek feedback from volunteers about their program.

Many organizations returned incomplete surveys, which may indicate a widespread lack of statistic gathering and record keeping in shelter volunteer programs.

Certainly, more research is needed. Animal shelters are in a wonderful position to take advantage of what their volunteers have to offer. Most shelters are getting there, and with a little assistance, shelter volunteer programs can blossom.

Introduction

Books on general volunteer management fill the shelves at bookstores, but they are not specific to animal care organizations. The HSUS has created this specialized manual to fill that void. Its information and advice are drawn from many sources in volunteer management and animal care and control. It is designed to help you get the volunteer assistance you need—not only to provide care for the six to eight million animals entering U.S. shelters each year, but also to become a positive force for change in your community. What better way to help stem the tide of animal homelessness than to involve your community in the process? That's what volunteers are for!

Aren't They Supposed to Save Us Time?

Whether you manage an animal shelter, humane society, or animal control agency or oversee a volunteer program in such an organization, you may have asked yourself: "Why all the bother with management details? Volunteers are supposed to be helping us, not creating more work, right?" But the details are what make a program successful. You just have to learn how to persuade volunteers that it's worth their while to donate time to your organization and maximize their productivity while they are with you. Once a volunteer program is up and running, the benefits will outweigh your initial investment.

Volunteers are people just like you. They're busy with families, jobs, and personal commitments. While they may care about your cause, they need to feel that the time they donate is well spent. Remember, it's relatively easy to recruit volunteers but much more difficult to keep them motivated and productive.

To attract and retain volunteers, your organization will need to do some legwork. Good programs can't be launched on a whim; effective volunteer management requires careful planning, adequate monetary and human resources, and strong leadership.

The results of the landmark study *Managing Volunteers: A Report from United Parcel Service* (UPS Foundation 1998) proved what many have suspected all along: if you want your volunteer program to succeed, you first need to get your house in order. The national random telephone survey of 1,030 people and an additional 1,400 interviews in seven major metropolitan areas revealed some interesting findings:

- The number-one reason for leaving volunteer positions (cited by 65 percent of respondents) was that volunteers had more important demands on their time.

- Two-fifths of respondents (38 percent) said they would like to do more volunteer work, and three-fifths (58 percent) said they'd be more likely to volunteer if organizations made good use of their time.

- Half of respondents (52 percent) said they would be likely to volunteer for an organization that "has a reputation for being well managed."

- Two out of five volunteers (40 percent) stopped volunteering for an organization at some point because of poor volunteer management practices—in particular, because the organization itself was not well managed or did not make good use of volunteer time.

- One out of four (26 percent) stopped volunteer work because the organization itself was not well managed, and 23 percent felt the organization did not make good use of their time.

"The findings reflect that the American public sees the inefficient management of volunteer time as a basic obstacle to increased volunteerism," wrote the researchers (UPS Foundation 1998, 1). "Time is the most limiting factor in volunteering, and volunteers expect the time they donate to be well managed. The findings substantiate a crisis in volunteer management. Too many potential and active volunteers are turned off by what they regard as inefficient use of their time."

There *is* a large pool of willing volunteers. According to *Giving and Volunteering in the United States* (Independent Sector 2001), 44 percent of people over the age of twenty-one volunteered with a formal organization in 2000. That's almost half of all adults in the United States. Even more encouraging was that, of those volunteers, 69 percent reported they volunteered regularly—once a month or more often.

To complete its 2002 survey, the First Side Partners consulting group asked nonprofit managers to identify the main reason their volunteer programs were successful (Lindberg and Dooley 2002). The majority said that their success was based on providing meaningful work—work that supported the mission of the organization—to volunteers. In addition, they felt they had integrated volunteers into the organization so completely that they did not think they could carry out their mission without the volunteers' help.

"In a large number of instances, respondents said that the support and commitment of the administration and leadership was essential to their success," wrote the authors of the First Side Partners report. "The other area that came up frequently was that it was important to have dedicated, professional staff assigned to the volunteer program" (Lindberg and Dooley 2002, 18).

Table 4

People Would Be More Likely to Volunteer If the Volunteer Organization...

Description	Percent
Made good use of time	58
Had reputation of being well managed	52
Made better use of talents	50
Made tasks more clearly defined	41
Offered experience that helped career	39
Offered thanks	31

Providing a well-managed volunteer program that makes the best use of a volunteer's time is crucial to attracting—and keeping—the volunteers you need.

Source: UPS Foundation 1998.

How to Use This Manual

Remember that volunteer programs need to be developed in stages. You probably can't tackle everything in this manual right away. That's fine: start with the basics and work your way through over time. Consider reading this manual through once, then referring to the chapters you need as you build your volunteer program.

Another note: although this manual focuses primarily on those organizations that operate animal shelters, the information presented here can help any animal care organization.

Chapter 1

Deciding if You're Ready for Volunteers

Your organization may already be using volunteer help in some way. But chances are, if you're reading this manual, things aren't perfect, and your volunteer program could use a boost. Whether you already have volunteers involved or you're just getting started, it's important to determine how prepared your organization is for volunteers who are ready to give their time and talents.

Volunteers can be wonderful assets to your organization. They can work within and beyond your shelter's walls—raising needed funds, providing administrative support, fostering animals, counseling adopters, and socializing animals. They can also be a vital link between your organization and the community you serve. As ambassadors for your organization, they reach a lot of people in the community—their family, friends, co-workers, and others. However, volunteers are not simply free help; they require an investment of valuable staff time. The success of your volunteer program relies on a strong foundation. You will need to establish boundaries within which your volunteers can operate and develop a decision-making chain of command. Thoughtful, strong leadership and a system that helps volunteers support the organization—not control it—are critical. Adding volunteers to a disorganized or problem-ridden sheltering operation will only serve to make things worse. You risk doing damage to your programs and your organization's reputation if you bring in volunteers before you're ready to work with them.

This prospect shouldn't deter you from using volunteers, but it should serve as a reminder to proceed thoughtfully and take a critical look at how your organization operates. Be sure to clean your house before you invite in the guests by conducting a self-evaluation to determine your organization's stability.

Conducting an Organizational "Self-Evaluation"

Use the following checklist to help you determine how ready your organization is for volunteers.

- **Do you have good staff retention rates?** If not, why are staff leaving? Are staff members frustrated by a lack of support? Are internal politics causing a rift?

- **Have you covered the basics?** Do you have an efficient cage-cleaning process and sound disease-control protocols or are you struggling with basic sanitation issues and constant illness outbreaks in the shelter? Unless basic operations are in order, adding volunteers is bound to make matters worse—volunteers will no doubt spread the word in the community that the shelter is not run well, thereby damaging your reputation. Make sure you are operating efficiently and effectively so that you can welcome volunteers and bring them into the fold.

■ **Do you have written standard operating procedures (SOPs) that both staff and volunteers adhere to?** (Even the smallest operation benefits from written SOPs. The HSUS offers a free template of SOPs that can be modified to fit any sheltering operation.)

■ **Do you have a strategic plan that maps out your organization's future?** You should have a written strategic plan that includes a needs assessment and your organization's mission, goals, objectives, and action items. The plan should be measurable—with concrete steps for completion. If you already use volunteers, consider including a few volunteer representatives in the strategic planning process. Knowing your goals for the future will help you recruit worthy volunteers to your cause and help you determine which projects need the most help from volunteers.

■ **Do you have written job descriptions for your staff?** They are a must—and an important first step before creating job descriptions for your volunteers.

■ **Do you provide regular performance evaluations to your staff?** Are staff members accountable for their work? To succeed, both staff members and volunteers need feedback, positive and negative. An up-and-running performance evaluation program for staff will help you lay the groundwork for evaluating volunteers as well.

■ **Do you conduct orientations for new staff?** All staff should receive a thorough introduction to your organization that includes its history and philosophy. Such orientations should also address the importance of volunteers to your organization and explain how staff can work well with them. For a volunteer program to be successful, staff must see how much the organization benefits from donated time.

■ **Do you have space allocated for volunteers?** They need room to work, a place to store their supplies, and a place to take a break when needed, such as a shared staff-volunteer lounge.

■ **Does the public view your organization positively?** Consider inviting in a "mystery shopper"—perhaps a friend or someone you know who has never visited your shelter and doesn't have any experience in animal care and control. Ask the person to stop by unannounced and make mental notes of his or her impressions. Is the building inviting? Are the cages clean? Are the animals healthy? Is the staff friendly, or is the facility smelly, dreary, and depressing? First impressions are lasting and can mean the difference between keeping or losing volunteers as well as community support.

■ **Are you communicating your decisions about animal dispositions clearly and honestly to the public?** Do you explain the agency's behavior evaluation program, its holding procedures, and its method of euthanasia? Are you open about your adoption process and other service programs, or does the community feel your organization is secretive and closed-off? If your agency is already talking openly about even the touchiest issues, it's hard for anyone to stir up controversy. Honest communication helps shelters earn the trust of their communities.

■ **Does your organization regularly receive positive media attention?** If not, and if the media have been critical of your operation, take a look at the reasons behind the accusations and work to repair the organization's reputation before recruiting volunteers. Negative media attention will certainly make potential volunteers leery of donating time to your organization.

■ **Are you using sodium pentobarbital injection by well-trained staff members as your method of euthanasia?** How are euthanasia decisions made? In most cases, volunteers should not be directly involved in the euthanasia process, but you can count on their asking lots of questions, including ones about your decision-making process and euthanasia method. As long as both of these are humane, you'll be able to explain and defend what you do to anyone who asks.

■ **Have you analyzed your community's most pressing issues?** How is your organization addressing them? Are feral cats a great concern? Are low-cost spay/neuter services lacking? Assessing local needs will help you develop a plan for achieving your goal of resolving community animal problems. Focusing on these issues will help your organization appeal to local volunteers affected by these concerns.

■ **Is your shelter located in a safe area?** If not, you may need to take precautions to ensure staff and volunteers are not endangered coming and going for their shifts. (Chapter 9 discusses risk management.)

Resolve any existing problems with your current volunteer program before you expand volunteer recruitment. The middle of a crisis is not a good time to bring volunteers on board. Your organization is likely to be attractive in the wrong way to the wrong type of person if you recruit during a crisis. Such volunteers may think they need to take over and fix your problems rather than help you achieve your mission.

If you need help with any of these issues before bringing volunteers on board, The HSUS is available to provide assistance. You can also take advantage of local resources: if you're struggling with basic issues such as cleaning and disease control, for example, consider recruiting a veterinarian from your community as your first volunteer. Perhaps you'll find a veterinarian willing to look at your cleaning and health care protocols and make recommendations for improvement.

Remember that developing good programs is a process that takes time and should be done in stages. Take it slowly and work on one area at a time. The most successful shelters operate like businesses. Your organization, regardless of its size, should be no different.

Deciding if You're Ready for Volunteers

Can an Organization Succeed Without Volunteers?

Volunteer programs may not be feasible for all agencies. Liability concerns and labor issues are enough to make some animal care and control agencies shy away from placing volunteers in positions of responsibility. Humane organizations that lack the resources necessary to oversee volunteers may also decide against recruiting donated assistance. A shelter certainly can be successful without volunteers, but if you decide not to incorporate volunteers into your operation, know that you are missing out on an important opportunity. Volunteers not only can provide much needed support to the staff but they also increase morale by validating the shelter's work. Their opinions of the organization will travel through word of mouth and may carry more weight because of their affiliation with the organization. Because they are volunteers, the community may be even more willing to listen to them than to paid staff since they don't have a financial stake in presenting the agency in a favorable light. The more involved the public is with your issues, the more likely it is that the public will support your cause.

A volunteer program can help you build relationships with other organizations as well. For example, programs run by volunteers to assist the pets of domestic violence victims can help build bridges with human services agencies. Such relationships can generate leads to grant-making organizations or to local nonprofits that otherwise might not have considered you as a resource.

According to a 2001 Independent Sector report, volunteers are bigger donors than donors who do not volunteer. Its survey found that households in which the respondent also volunteered gave substantially more than did households in which the respondent did not volunteer. For giving households, the average contributions were $2,295 from volunteers and $1,009 from nonvolunteers.

Free help and free money? To get the benefit of this double blessing, you must first allocate some time and money of your own to get your volunteer program operating successfully.

Figure 1
Giving History of Volunteers and Non-Volunteers

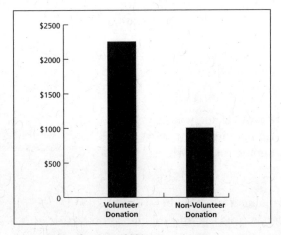

Source: Independent Sector 2001.

Figure 2
Types of Organizations to which Volunteers Choose to Donate Their Time, in Percentages

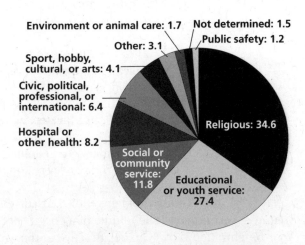

Nationally, very few volunteers are selecting animal welfare or environmental organizations for their volunteer work. If animal care organizations provide strong management and structure to their volunteer programs, they will see a steady increase in volunteer participation and will reap the many benefits these dedicated individuals have to offer.

Source: U.S. Department of Labor, Bureau of Labor Statistics 2003.

Budgeting for a Volunteer Program

Volunteers are not "free help." To provide necessary structure, training, and support, you will need to create a budget for the volunteer program. If you believe volunteers will compensate for staffing shortages, think again. Preexisting managerial and financial problems cannot be solved simply by adding volunteers.

"Do you have money available that you did not have to spend because you utilized volunteers? Hardly," writes Susan Ellis (1996, 11). "Much more accurate is the recognition that volunteers *allow you to spend every dollar you have—and then do more*. Volunteers extend the budget [emphasis in the original]." That's the beautiful thing about volunteers: they allow you to expand your programs and provide more services.

While the costs involved certainly don't have to break the bank, you will need to allocate some monetary resources to ensure the program has what it needs to thrive. First Side Partners (Lindberg and Dooley 2002, 26–27) found that the presence of a budget for the volunteer program

> [I]s clearly one of the key indications of an organization's commitment to its volunteers, since budgeting for volunteer staffing, recognition, support materials, and other expenses is critical to the organization's ability to adequately support a solid volunteer program. And...it also sends a more positive message to volunteers if the organization feels that volunteer work is important enough to warrant dedicated funding.

A line-item budget increases respect for the volunteer program. Volunteers are a valuable fund-raising source, since they can help you plan successful fund-raising events. A good volunteer program can often raise money to cover its own expenses.

What should you include in your budget for your volunteer program?

- **Insurance.** Does your current organizational insurance policy cover volunteers? If not, you will need to add volunteer coverage to the policy, which may increase the program's overall cost.

- **Staffing.** Who will develop all the necessary tools for the program? Who will supervise the volunteers and their orientations? Even if you have a current staff member to manage the volunteers, determine what percentage of his or her time will be spent overseeing the program and include that dollar equivalent in the volunteer program budget. If a position needs to be created, look for funding possibilities. Fort Wayne (Indiana) Animal Care and Control was able to secure grant money to cover the cost of the full-time volunteer coordinator's salary for three years.

- **Equipment.** What tools will volunteers need? If they'll be doing data entry, is there a workstation available? Do volunteers have a phone to use during their shift? Do they have the appropriate supplies? If they will be walking dogs, do you have enough leashes and plastic bags for cleanup? Many of these items can be solicited from donors if you think ahead and you prepare for volunteers before they start flowing through your doors.

■ **Office Supplies.** The volunteer coordinator will need supplies for running the program and printing materials for recruitment, training, communication, and recognition. E-mail has certainly provided an economical way to keep in touch with volunteers and should be used as much as possible, but be sure to budget for postage and stationery for the handwritten thank-you notes that show volunteers how much you appreciate them.

■ **Volunteer Identification.** What will volunteers be required to wear? Will they need name tags? What about volunteer aprons or T-shirts? It's important for volunteers to be clearly identified. Some shelters have avoided this expense by asking volunteers to purchase the "volunteer" T-shirt or apron as a one-time fee. However, you should always budget for extras in case a volunteer can't afford it—no volunteer should be turned away because he or she doesn't have money.

■ **Volunteer Expense Reimbursements.** If a volunteer uses his or her own car to transport animals to off-site adoption events, will the volunteer be reimbursed for mileage? Most volunteer programs provide compensation for such tasks. While many volunteers may decline the offer, money should still be available to cover such expenses.

Don't think of these expenses as "money down the drain"; view them as an investment. Volunteer involvement in a well-run program will provide a wonderful return, helping you help more animals in a better way.

Chapter 2

Developing Good Staff-Volunteer Relationships

*It is not enough to treat volunteers like staff;
we must also treat staff like volunteers!*
—I.H. Scheier (1993, 1)

It All Starts with Good Leadership

Before you can bring volunteers on board, it's critical that staff and management be 100 percent supportive of a volunteer program. If staff can't—or won't—work with volunteers, how can you expect volunteers to work for your organization?

The commitment to volunteer involvement has to come from the highest levels of the organization. The board of directors and executive director in a nonprofit organization, or the municipal governing body in a public agency, should require development of detailed policies and procedures to guide a volunteer program.

The leadership role of the executive director or CEO in creating a supportive environment for a volunteer program is essential, according to Lindberg and Dooley (2002, 20). "In the programs where the CEO was solidly behind the involvement of volunteers, managers felt that this involvement was of tremendous benefit to their ability to recruit and retain good volunteers, and some felt it was the single most important factor in their success," they concluded.

The top-level leadership of an organization can help set the tone and create a positive environment for a volunteer program if you:

■ Conduct a strategic planning process in which all staff determine where the organization is heading and discuss how volunteers can help meet goals.

■ Dedicate a staff person—ideally a full-time director of volunteers—to oversee and manage the program.

■ Require good structure and policies that will guide volunteer activities.

■ Use volunteer help yourself. For example, the executive director can have a volunteer assistant or use volunteers on special projects he or she is coordinating.

■ Interact with volunteers regularly by participating in orientations, attending recognition events, and being available for questions during volunteer hours.

- Incorporate "working with volunteers" into staff job descriptions.

- Make sure that staff needs are being met first. (See the earlier discussion of written job descriptions and staff recognition.)

- Train staff to supervise and work with volunteers.

- Reward staff who work well with volunteers.

- Incorporate volunteers into the organizational chart.

Staff Commitment to the Volunteer Program

Volunteers need to be woven into the fabric of the organization, but integration of volunteers depends on a welcoming staff who see the benefits of volunteer help. It is crucial that staff and volunteers have mutual respect and see themselves as part of a team working together for the benefit of animals and the community. This is often easier said than done.

You can't force volunteers on the staff. If time isn't devoted to structuring the program, the staff won't perceive the volunteers as being necessary to their success. In fact, quite the opposite will occur. Staff will view volunteers as simply another "task" added to their already overburdened workloads. Worse yet, the volunteers who are brought in will feel unwelcome, unvalued, and not needed—and they'll leave.

Consider the experience of an Ohio shelter volunteer who witnessed such alienation firsthand:

> While the shelter says they want volunteers, the staff regards most volunteers as "in the way." There is very little guidance and even less delegation of duties. Perhaps due to insufficient training and unfriendly staff, most volunteers do not stay around very long. If you would ask the staff to name—first name only— more than five volunteers, they could not do it. I think that's a shame. (Personal communication)

This is not an uncommon scenario in shelters where the volunteer programs have been developed without input and buy-in from the staff. "'It's easier to do it myself' is a death sentence for the volunteer program, when pronounced by staff who sincerely believe it," writes I.H. Scheier (1993, 16). He acknowledges, however, that the urge to avoid delegating is understandable, especially in the beginning stages of the program. Staff may put in an hour or two for each hour they receive in return from volunteers.

"That's to be expected," he explains.

> But, when things settle down, you should normally expect to get back at least 10–15 hours of work from volunteers for every hour you invest in them. In some programs, the payoff can get as high as 100 to 1 or even 200 to 1. (16)

Volunteers may have misconceptions as well. They may think that because a staff member receives a paycheck, he or she doesn't care as much as the dedicated volunteer does. Education and mutual respect are key to understanding. Volunteers need to understand the work that goes on in the shelter, particularly the difficulties the staff face, and they need to be supportive and respectful. It's critical to avoid an "us against them" environment.

To help build a good relationship, make sure you provide balanced praise: rather than praise only the work of volunteers, praise the combined team efforts of staff and volunteers. Not only will that motivate staff and volunteers; it will also help strengthen the relationship between them. Keep track of what your volunteers do for you and how much money they donate and generate. Sharing such information with the staff will help build acceptance and appreciation. (For more information on tracking your volunteers, see chapter 7.)

Finding the right balance and developing positive staff-volunteer relationships is important. "There may be no factor within your program that impacts retention more quickly and obviously than relationships volunteers and paid staff have with each other," says Sue Vineyard, contributor to *Grapevine*, a newsletter for volunteer managers (2000, 15). "People simply stay longer in situations where they enjoy their co-workers and others they encounter." Consider these two hypothetical (but all too common) scenarios:

Scenario #1

"We've tried the volunteer route, and it's never paid off. Volunteers just don't know what they're doing, and my staff complains that, although these volunteers mean well, they just get in the way. My operations manager doesn't have time to deal with them. Plus, they create problems by mixing up the cage cards and giving visitors the wrong information. We always have too many volunteers on Saturday and not enough volunteers during the week. And they just don't seem to stick around very long. It just doesn't seem like the time we're spending on this program is worth it."

—*Executive Director, Troubled Waters Animal Shelter*

Scenario #2

"Our volunteers have been a blessing to our operation. They've been involved in almost every aspect of what we do and have helped our paid staff tremendously. The staff seems to really enjoy the volunteers' company and assistance. The program our volunteer coordinator has set up is top-notch, and the people she brings in seem to really enjoy their work. I think it gives them a strong sense of accomplishment. Our volunteers have helped us expand our outreach program. I don't know what we'd do without them."

—*Executive Director, Sunshine Animal Shelter*

If you see yourself in Scenario #1, here are steps to developing strong staff-volunteer relations:

Step 1. Conduct a strategic planning process with the entire staff—and a few volunteer representatives, if you have them. If you've never done strategic planning before, there are plenty of resources available to help you. Humane Society University (*www.HumaneSocietyU.org*) offers an online course in strategic planning. Visit *www.boardsource.org* (select "strategic planning" from the topic search drop-down menu for a host of helpful tools) or see Recommended Reading.

As part of the strategic planning process, have the staff help identify services that need improvement. Determine what services or programs staff would love to offer but haven't had time to implement. Don't rush the process. Strategic planning is intensive and time-consuming, but your organization will benefit tremendously overall. And it will make the staff—and ultimately the volunteers you recruit—more effective.

Step 2. Discuss how volunteers can improve existing services and make new ones possible. Proceed slowly and listen to staff's concerns about volunteer assistance. The staff's attitude toward volunteers—positive or negative—will come through loud and clear. Talking to staff about some of the benefits of working with volunteers may help. These benefits include:

- By supervising and working with volunteers, staff can gain valuable supervisory experience that will look great on a resume.

- Staff will have a say in what volunteers do and in development of volunteer-related policies.

- Volunteers can help free up staff time spent on daily tasks, allowing staff to focus on larger organizational goals.

- When volunteers, as members of the community, see firsthand the challenges staff face at animal shelters, they may become more supportive. Such support may help staff feel less isolated from the public and feel their work validated.

If the potential for these benefits is still not enough to gain staff support for a volunteer program, up the ante. The Dumb Friends League in Denver, Colorado, goes the extra mile and actually offers an additional $.50 an hour as an incentive for staff members willing to work with and supervise volunteers. Such an approach is sure to be popular with staff in any community!

Step 3. Encourage staff to share their concerns. Talk specifically about the challenges staff face in working with volunteers. More than likely, you'll hear at least some of the following common concerns:

- Volunteers will make mistakes.

- Volunteers will be valued more than staff.

- Volunteers will question staff decisions about difficult issues such as adoptions and euthanasia.

- If volunteers do well, they may replace staff.

- Volunteers will spy on staff and will be critical of their work.

- Volunteers are untrained people who need to be assigned simple tasks.

Although many of these fears are misconceptions, some are valid. Volunteers *will* make mistakes if they aren't trained properly. They *may* question staff decisions if the reasons aren't explained up front. To help ease these concerns, explain how upper management will create the necessary orientation and training program to prevent these problems.

Step 4. Define policies that address concerns of both staff and volunteers. Key staff should be included in a policy-creating working group. If your shelter already has volunteers, be sure to include them, too. Giving staff and volunteers a voice in policy development helps them accept new rules and structure rather than resent new policies suddenly thrust on them.

How can developing policies reduce staff concerns and prevent misunderstandings with volunteers? Take this example: your staff resents constant questions from volunteers about the status of certain animals—why one was euthanized or another was excluded from colony housing. Certainly, volunteers should be able to ask such questions, but it may work best if one staff member—perhaps the volunteer coordinator—serves as the point person for them. With such a buffer, staff who are directly involved in euthanasia decisions and other difficult tasks are less likely to feel as though volunteers are confronting or second-guessing them.

Step 5. Provide staff with a "safety zone" away from volunteers. At the Humane Society at Lollypop Farm, in Rochester, New York, staff were becoming frustrated by volunteers showing up early in the morning, before the shelter opened. Staff wanted a chance to start their day and drink their coffee without the volunteers asking them questions. Maggie Huff, the volunteer coordinator, stepped in and required volunteers to adhere to the shelter's hours for the public. Staff members greatly appreciated the quiet time and were ready for volunteers when the shelter doors opened. Paying close attention to staff needs can go a long way toward keeping the peace.

Can Volunteers Replace Paid Staff?

An organization's decision to bring in volunteers may spark fears that volunteers could eventually replace staff. After all, volunteers can do many of the same tasks staff do—and they aren't paid a salary. Why couldn't the organization simply look to the volunteers as an alternative to an expensive payroll?

In a well-run organization, staff have nothing to fear. Paying a salary provides the organization with more stability by requiring staff to be there at certain times and perform specific, and specialized, job functions. Volunteers, on the other hand, are afforded more flexibility in choosing what positions they'll fill and how many hours they'll work. And most volunteers hold full-time jobs elsewhere—they can't fulfill the responsibilities of full-time staff when they can donate only a few hours of their time. Ultimately, paid staff are essential to operating a full-scale shelter successfully.

Typically, in a thriving organization, an expanding volunteer program leads to the creation of new paid jobs as resources become available. In fact, many community animal welfare groups start out as all-volunteer-based but eventually add paid staff positions as their services and programs mature. Volunteers enable shelters to do more in the community, which increases donor support and demand for the programs, which result in paid positions. In other words, an effective volunteer program usually leads to more paid staff, not fewer!

Chapter 3

Determining the Role of Volunteers

Volunteers want and deserve meaningful jobs, not just busy work that staff doesn't want to do. In fact, volunteers can do much of the same work as staff. First Side Partners found that organizations are much more effective in carrying out their missions with the help of volunteers when few tasks are considered "staff only." "Instead, volunteers are considered unpaid staff, recruited as valuable members of the team, and given meaningful and challenging work," write the study's authors (Lindberg and Dooley, 2002, 13). "The result is astounding: some organizations receive nearly half a million donated hours of work, the equivalent of 250 full-time paid employees!"

Here are just a few areas in which volunteers can provide meaningful assistance:

Adoption Counseling	Humane Education
Clerical (data entry, filing, typing)	Animal Care
Customer Service (receptionist)	Veterinary Assistance
Foster Care	Gift Shop Management
Socialization of Dogs/Dog Walking	Fund-Raising
Socialization of Cats	Special Events
Small-Mammal Companionship	Community Outreach
Dog Training	Animal-Assisted Therapy

What to Consider When Developing Volunteer Positions

If you are developing a new volunteer program, begin by offering just a couple of volunteer positions. As the program grows, slowly add new and more responsible positions. As you determine where your shelter's gaps and opportunities exist, decide which tasks can be handled by beginning volunteers, which can go to longtime volunteers, and which should be done by paid staff only. Consider these tips when creating volunteer positions:

■ **Volunteer positions should be needs-driven.** Staff usually know best what needs to be done and will accept more readily volunteers whose work helps staff directly. When working with staff to develop volunteer opportunities, first consider the most pressing concerns of the organization. Brainstorm with the staff about things they would love to do but have never had the time to do themselves. Their ideas can be turned into volunteer positions.

■ **Free up staff time for other projects.** You can also ask staff to identify the parts of their job they don't like. Volunteer positions may be created to cover those things thereby freeing staff time to move onto other, more satisfying projects. This approach will certainly help win points with the staff and may help facilitate good staff-volunteer relations. Do not, however, create a volunteer position solely to do the mundane tasks staff doesn't want or you'll likely lose a worthy volunteer.

■ **Create entry-level positions.** Start your volunteers out with entry-level positions such as dog walking and cat care. Then allow them to move up through the ranks into more complex positions such as adoption counseling or veterinary assistance. Volunteers enjoy opportunities to grow and advance—and assigning them such responsibilities gives you the opportunity to recognize good volunteers with a promotion.

■ **Make the volunteer assignments meaningful.** You need to create a job that volunteers will actually want to do. They aren't getting a paycheck, so the work needs to be interesting and rewarding so volunteers continue doing it. Set high expectations for your volunteers and don't be afraid to challenge them. Assign volunteers tasks and activities that are truly important—don't assign work that is boring or too easy.

That isn't to say you can't have your volunteers assist with menial tasks such as bulk mailings or data entry. But it must be clear to the volunteer why the task is important and how it benefits the organization. For example, if volunteers are asked to stuff envelopes for a bulk mailing, make sure they understand that the mailing is an appeal to donors that will fund a new program to treat injured animals. It needs to be clear that volunteer involvement in the project may result in raising hundreds or thousands of dollars needed to help the animals.

Prospective volunteers also need to understand that volunteering for the local animal welfare organization does not necessarily mean playing with puppies and kittens all day. There is other work to be done as well. The work needs to be rewarding to the volunteer, but it also must fill a specific need of the organization and the broader community. At the Dumb Friends League, volunteers are required to help clean up after the animals. Dog walkers must also clean the kennels to ensure that all the work gets done. Combining these tasks eliminates situations where volunteers just play with the animals and avoid the harder but equally important work that must be done.

■ **Make it fun.** If you have an important job that is not particularly fun, be creative! Several years ago, the volunteer coordinator at the Peninsula Humane Society in California was having a hard time recruiting volunteers for the lost-and-found program. To reunite lost pets with their owners as quickly as possible, the shelter needed help in its daily checks of lost reports against the animals in the kennels. But the job was a bit boring, and volunteers just weren't interested in it.

With a little creative brainstorming, the volunteer coordinator revamped the position and developed the "Super Sleuth" contest. Each volunteer recruited to the program was given the job title of "pet detective" and the assignment was to match as many lost-pet reports to stray pets arriving at the shelter as possible. The volunteer who reunited the most pets with their owners at the end of the month was named "best detective."

The result: Volunteers became quite competitive and turned an otherwise tedious volunteer job into a fun competition.

■ **Assign projects that can be completed in shorter time periods.** Keep in mind that individual volunteers typically contribute fewer hours per week than even part-time staff. According to UPS Foundation research (1998), 58 percent of the volunteers surveyed indicated they volunteer between one and five hours per month. Only 4 percent of the adult population reported volunteering more than 25 hours per month. Most volunteers are able to donate only a few hours per month, which presents a challenge for volunteer managers.

According to Safrit and Merril (2002), recent data show that while more people volunteer, fewer volunteers contribute a constant number of hours. "Organizations must find ways to structure volunteer work that will allow people greater flexibility to move in and out of volunteering as work and family pressures affect their lives," suggest the authors:

> Volunteer positions may need to be redesigned into smaller work segments that can be shared by two or more people. . . . More attention needs to be given to personal and professional development opportunities for volunteers that will increase individual effectiveness while maintaining personal interest. Job sharing and team volunteering would encourage longer-term individual volunteer commitments with shared responsibility. (14)

■ **Be flexible to accommodate more volunteers.** The more variety you can offer potential volunteers, the better luck you'll have recruiting them. Consider how many volunteer assignments can be completed beyond the shelter walls— and outside normal business hours. Do you need volunteers to make follow-up calls after adoption? Do you need to have your quarterly newsletters folded and labeled for mailing? These tasks may be completed easily from a volunteer's home during nonbusiness hours. Allowing such flexibility can result in greater participation and skirt the problem of trying to accomplish everything during the hours your facility is open.

■ **Remember that not all positions need to be animal related.** There are many positions volunteers can fill that have nothing to do with caring for animals. Data entry, web site development, and publication design are all great opportunities to involve volunteers who may not be able to handle the emotional aspects of the hands-on animal work in the shelter environment.

■ **Create resume-building positions that volunteers can use to find a paid job.** Many volunteers try a new volunteer position to gain experience and build a resume—an especially popular goal in a downward economy. Developing volunteer positions that include resume builders such as newsletter editing or computer data entry will help volunteers grow professionally as well as encourage greater participation in your program.

■ **Pace your volunteers.** Some come in raring to go and want to take on several positions, but they may end up committing themselves to more than they can handle. Channel that enthusiasm into one well-matched assignment at a time to ensure success.

Table 5.

A Snapshot of Volunteers in the United States, 2003

Description	Population Share
Number of people age sixteen and over who volunteered	63.8 million (28.8 percent of U.S. population)
Women volunteered more often than men	Women 32.2 percent; Men 25.1 percent
Median hours a volunteer spent volunteering	52 hours in 2003
Seniors donated the most median hours	88 hours in 2003
25–34 year olds donated the fewest median hours	36 hours in 2003

The typical volunteer contributed just 52 hours in 2003—one hour per week. Organizations can best attract and keep volunteers by offering volunteer positions that can be performed in short shifts.

Source: The Urban Institute 2004.

Now Put It in Writing

Once you've determined what your volunteers will do for you, develop written job descriptions for each volunteer position you want to fill just as you would for paid staff. A volunteer should be given an opportunity to read his or her job description and understand exactly what is expected. Keep in mind that the job description needs to be measurable. This will be the basis for evaluating whether your volunteers succeed in their commitment to your organization.

As an objective tool, a written job description reduces the chance of discrimination and provides a level of protection for the organization when problems arise with volunteer performance. It provides volunteers with a clear idea of what's expected and what needs to be done and gives staff clear guidance regarding what volunteers can and cannot do. A written job description is extremely helpful in situations where a volunteer isn't doing what he or she should be doing. When the performance is based on a written job description, there is little room for argument.

If you already have volunteers, but you aren't using job descriptions, ask your volunteers to help write their own. Involving volunteers in the process of creating structure for the program will help reduce resistance from volunteers who have been allowed to do whatever they want without any guidelines.

While you don't have to conform to this outline, each written job description should include the following information:

- Title

- Purpose of the position and how it helps the organization

- Supervisor

- Qualifications

- Physical requirements (e.g., ability to lift fifty-pound bags of dog food)

- Duties and responsibilities (be specific and write out the steps of the job involved)

- Training requirements

- Location of the job (at the shelter, from home, at off-site adoption center, etc.)

- Benefits to the volunteer

- Time commitment required

- Dress code required

When writing volunteer job descriptions, make sure that what's written accurately reflects what needs to be done. Consider "testing" your written job descriptions. Perform the job yourself and see if it matches the description committed to paper.

Be sure to use clear language and explain any unfamiliar terminology in the job description. Volunteers may be new to the field and may not understand certain terms particular to animal care and control. Each piece of the job description should be backed up by a written SOP or written instructions.

The following pages contain some sample job descriptions to help you develop your own. Once you've created the description, don't just hand it to the volunteer and tell him or her to get to work. Volunteers need to be taught *how* to do the job. Without proper volunteer training, you risk damaging your reputation if they make mistakes. You must develop *all* of the pieces of the program to produce happy, well-trained volunteers. The next few chapters give the secrets you need for success.

6317 Kyle Ave., P.O. Box 272450, Ft. Collins CO 80527
(970) 266-3647 Fax: (970) 226-2968
www.larimerhumane.org

Adoption Counselor

Major Objective: Introduce potential adopters to animals
that will complement the family's lifestyle.

Duties

■ Socialize and exercise adoption animals.

■ Maintain sanitary kennel environment by practicing good disease control protocol.

■ Professional approach to handling the animals and dealing with the public.

■ Escort families to a meeting area with an animal where you can discuss specific
or general behavior issues.

■ Oversee meeting between the individual/s and the animal/s to make sure
everyone seems to get along.

■ Answer questions about an individual animal that a client may have.

■ Escort clients through adoption areas pointing out specific animals
that may be suitable for their lifestyle.

■ Positively represent the Society's beliefs and philosophies.

Training

■ Attend a Volunteer Information Session

■ Complete Volunteer Application

■ Interview with Volunteer Coordinator

■ Attend Kennel Assistant Training

■ Attend Adoption Counseling Training

Commitment: Adoption Counselor volunteers act as kennel assistants with advanced training
and are asked to maintain their normal kennel assistant schedule of 1 two-hour shift per week.

Volunteer Profile: Engaging, outgoing self-starter. Individual must be willing to learn about
animal behavior and enjoy working with people as much as animals. An individual who wishes
to promote adoptions.

Volunteer Benefits

■ Chance to meet and interact with our invaluable adopters.

■ Extremely rewarding experience of sending an animal into a new home.

■ Direct contribution to increase in adoptions.

■ Learn information that will improve your relationship with your own companion animal.

Supervision: Direct supervision by Volunteer Coordinator; Indirect supervision
by Animal Care supervisor.

What Humane Society Volunteers Do

Meet and Greet

The goal of the volunteer program in Meet and Greet is to represent the Humane Society, respond to inquiries and requests for help, and guide visitors.

Requirements:
Ability and desire to represent the Humane Society.
Knowledge of H.S. programs and services.
Verbal communication skills.

Training:
The required training includes:
Basic—safety, health and guidelines.
H.S. history and programs.
How to use the phone/intercom/paging system.
Sources of information at the front desk.

Tasks:
Retrieve messages and route to staff.
Greet and direct visitors during shelter hours.
Relieve receptionist for daily inventory (a.m.)
Look up animal/person info on Chameleon.
Answer phone and provide info/referrals.
Take lost dog/cat reports.

Schedule:
Any two hour block between 10 a.m. and 5 p.m. weekends.

Advanced volunteers:
Train for behavior help line.

The Humane Society of Rochester
& Monroe County at Lollypop Farm
99 Victor Road
Fairport, NY 14450
585-223-1330
www.lollypop.org

VOLUNTEER ASSIGNMENT

TITLE

Animal Behavior Head Start Assistant—AB-HDST

MAJOR OBJECTIVE

To assist the Head Start Instructors in teaching basic obedience commands to shelter dogs. The Head Start Program's objective is to make the League's bouncy, adolescent dogs more manageable, more adoptable, and more likely to stay in their new homes.

RESPONSIBILITIES

1. Following established procedures, work with Shelter dogs to teach them basic obedience commands. After training, Volunteer Head Start Assistants may begin work with the dogs of their own choosing, or may continue work with the dogs already in the program.

2. Keep detailed records (manually and through Chameleon database) of the progress of dogs worked with in the Head Start Program.

QUALIFICATIONS

1. Computer entry skills (Chameleon).

2. Comfort in working with dogs.

3. Some experience with basic obedience work preferred but not necessary.

TRAINING

1. Attend a 2-1/2 hour orientation program.

2. Interview with the Volunteer Services Manager or designee.

3. Attend an all-day training session covering the League's philosophies, policies and procedures.

4. Complete the 4-hour Head Start Class.

5. Complete an additional 3-hour training with Head Start Instructor, to include documentation procedures and commands not covered in the Head Start Class.

6. Suggested Reading: Karen Pryor's *Don't Shoot the Dog*.

continued...

TIME AND PLACE

Volunteer Head Start Assistants may work with dogs at either the Quebec location or the Extended Care Center. Hours may be chosen from hours of operation.

COMMITMENT

One 3-hour shift per week for a minimum of six months.

SUPERVISION

Responsible to staff Animal Behavior Supervisor. Indirect supervision by Volunteer Services Manager.

BENEFITS

1. Opportunity to represent the League.

2. Help make challenging and exuberant shelter dogs more adoptable and more likely to stay in their new homes.

3. Working directly with animals.

4. Continuing education programs.

5. Recognition events.

6. Excess insurance.

7. Two newsletters.

8. Reduced prices in our Pet Supply Area.

9. Personal satisfaction.

10. Licks and tail wags.

HAWAIIAN HUMANE SOCIETY

Volunteer Job Description

Cat Socializer

Job Summary: Socialize, train and groom cats

Time Commitment: 3 hours per week, 6-month minimum commitment

Supervisor: Animal Behavior Program Coordinator

Qualifications: Must be 18 years of age or older. Must have completed
6 months of volunteer service as a cat house caretaker.

Duties

1. Cat socializers will work with specific cats selected by the staff. Handle and groom
   the cat to make him/her more comfortable with being handled and being around people.
   For example, handle each paw and extend claws to prepare cat for having nails clipped.

2. Train and familiarize cat with a cat harness as time permits.

3. Train cats to perform simple tricks for treats, if time permits.

4. If a cat has special needs, ensure that visitors handle the cat properly to help
   both the visitor and cat have a safe and pleasant experience.

5. Fill out training and socialization log form for each cat handled during your shift.

6. Provide mentoring support to new cat house volunteers.

7. Make follow-up calls to adopters of cats in the socialization program.

Montgomery Humane Society's
Volunteer Job Description

Title: Office Assistant

Major Objective: To assist staff with administrative duties.

Responsibilities

1. General office duties: filing, typing, mail, answering telephone, etc.
2. Greet customers, answer telephone, provide accurate referral information.
3. Computer data entry.
4. Assist with additional projects when necessary.

Qualifications

1. Positive and friendly attitude.
2. Excellent telephone courtesy habits to include good listening and speaking skills.
3. Excellent appearance and common courtesy habits when dealing with customers.
4. Excellent handwriting—must be legible and concise.
5. Good office organization and accurate record-keeping skills.
6. Ability to perform many tasks at one time.
7. Minimum of 18 years of age.
8. Dedication to MHS philosophies.

Training

1. Attend orientation program.
2. Interview with the Volunteer Coordinator and other shelter directors.
3. Supervised on-the-job training with Office Manager or Volunteer Coordinator.

Time and Place

1. Scheduled shifts during hours of operation at the MHS facility, 1150 John Overton Drive.

Commitment

1. Minimum of one four-hour shift per month.
2. Three-month minimum.

Supervision

1. Direct supervision by the Montgomery Humane Society staff or appointed volunteer.

Benefits

1. Personal satisfaction and education.
2. Volunteer recognition awards and events.
3. Subscription to quarterly newsletter, *Pet Pause*.
4. Licks, purrs, and tail wags.
5. Improvement in communication, animal handling, and listening skills.

Chapter 4

Recruiting Volunteers

This manual covers recruitment here for sequential order, but your shelter must develop its *entire* program before bringing in new volunteers. Don't advertise for help until you can handle it.

Not sure if you're ready to begin recruiting? The following checklist adapted from McCurley and Lynch (1996) can help.

- Do all staff understand and accept the volunteers' roles?

- Have you consulted with staff who will supervise or work with volunteers?

- Is a complete and accurate job description written for each volunteer position?

- Do the position descriptions clearly identify the qualifications for the jobs and outline the purpose and nature of the work to be done?

- Have you identified a good working environment for the volunteers, in terms of workspace, equipment, etc.?

- Do you have a recruitment plan for seeking qualified applicants for the positions?

- Do you have a screening and interviewing process to distinguish qualified applicants from those who are unqualified?

- Do you know how you will handle unqualified applicants?

- Do you have a plan for orienting volunteers?

- Do you have a training program for volunteers?

- Do you have a plan for reviewing and promoting volunteers in the program?

- Have you addressed legal and insurance issues to protect volunteers and your shelter?

If you answered no to any of the previous questions, you still have work to do before starting recruitment. Rushing into recruitment before you are prepared will create a revolving door of volunteers because the program isn't well managed.

How do you find volunteers to do the jobs you've created? The key to recruitment is to find the *right* people for the *right* job. Don't be afraid to ask your community for help. According to Independent Sector, individuals who were asked to volunteer were much more likely to do so (71 percent) than were those who had not been asked (29 percent). Don't wait around for volunteers to find you. You need to be out in the community seeking the volunteers you need.

Competition for volunteer assistance is stiff, with the vast majority of volunteers donating their time to religious (43.4 percent), health care (18 percent), or educational (17.3 percent) organizations. The Independent Sector survey indicated that only 4.8 percent of people who volunteered during 2000 chose to donate their time to environmental or animal welfare organizations.

If interested volunteers aren't knocking down your doors, don't worry. There are lots of ways to recruit the volunteers you need. Here are just a few suggestions:

■ **Ask current volunteers to spread the word about your program and/or invite a friend or family member to your next new volunteer orientation.** Word of mouth can be a great advertising method. Once the word gets out that your organization is a great place to volunteer, you may find your recruitment efforts getting easier. Be sure to reward volunteers who recruit new volunteers to the organization!

■ **Blanket the community with a general call for volunteers.** Design a flier that includes basic information on the volunteer positions available, position requirements, minimum time commitments, contact names and numbers, and orientation schedules. (See the sample flier on page 27.) You can distribute the fliers in popular community locations or place similar ads in the newspaper. Ask a representative of your organization to speak to community groups, such as clubs and churches, about your organization. This can lead to lots of new volunteer recruits.

■ **Request the help of the media.** Contact local newspapers and television stations to see if they would be interested in doing a story on your volunteer program. If your local television station does a "pet of the week" segment, mention your volunteer needs during the spot or have a volunteer conduct the interview with his or her volunteer T-shirt clearly visible. Such coverage may help you find a batch of willing new volunteers.

Seattle Animal Shelter

Volunteer Orientation

Saturday, April 26th • 12:00PM • North Seattle Community College

The Seattle Animal Shelter's next Volunteer Orientation is scheduled for Saturday, April 26th at 12:00 p.m. in the Wellness Center Gym at North Seattle Community College. North Seattle Community College is located at 9600 College Way North, Seattle, 98103. For additional directions please visit www.northseattle.edu.

Volunteers must be at least 18 years old. All volunteers are required to attend this orientation. Shelter volunteers work at least 8 hours a month–this is a year round program, no seasonal volunteers please. We are looking for dedicated people who are serious about making a commitment to these animals. You will find working with the animals to be extremely rewarding. **Be a hero, save a life...volunteer.**

Volunteer programs include:

Advanced Off-site Dog Walking, Anti-Cruelty Program, Digital Photography, Dog Walking, Fabulous Felines, Foster Care, Furry 5K Race Team, Get Fit with Fido, Graphic Design, Grooming, Marketing/Fundraising, Matchmakers, 9-Lives, Pet Therapy, Special Events, Training/Cat Behavior, Training/Shelter Dogs

SEATTLE ANIMAL SHELTER VOLUNTEER PROGRAM

(206) 386-PETS • www.seattleanimalshelter.org
2061 15th Avenue West (1 mile South of the Ballard Bridge)

Open from 12:00pm - 6:00pm Tuesday - Saturday and 12:00pm - 4:00pm on Sunday

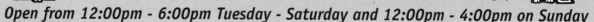

■ **Network, network, network!** Building relationships with other organizations in the community can provide big payoffs for your volunteer program. Learn your community's demographics and contact your local chamber of commerce. Visit with other nonprofits to see how you can help each other. You may be surprised by the resources you'll find in your own backyard!

■ **Harness the power of the Internet by advertising your volunteer positions on your organization's web site.** The following web sites invite organizations to post available volunteer positions, which are then easily searchable by zip code:

  • *www.PETS911.org*
  • *www.VolunteerMatch.org*
  • *www.SERVEnet.org*
  • *www.usafreedomcorps.gov*
  • *www.IdeaList.org*
  • *www.UnitedWay.org*

■ **Seek out the right volunteer for the job.** If you need dog walkers, post fliers advertising your dog-walking position at the local dog park or community gyms. In Lubbock, Texas, the animal services department and health education team jointly created "Walk-a-Hound, Lose-a-Pound," a volunteer dog-walking program that provides couch potato humans and stir-crazy pooches with some much needed exercise.

If you're looking for someone to teach humane education at elementary schools, contact the local Toastmaster's Club or individuals whose jobs require public speaking. Although time-consuming, these specialized searches are often more productive because the people targeted are most likely to enjoy and excel at the specific job.

■ **Register with the local volunteer center.** Many communities have volunteer centers that can match interested volunteers to specific positions within local nonprofits. For more information on volunteer centers, see page 30.

■ **Recruit groups of volunteers.** Many large companies promote volunteerism among their employees. They may even designate a day on which all interested employees can volunteer together on a project. Do your grounds need some upkeep? Consider working with a large corporation in your community to have a gardening day where volunteers from one company groom the lawn, plant flowers, and even paint the building's exterior.

Even other nonprofits can generate volunteers for your shelter. Community organizations such as churches may already have a large group of service-oriented people.

In fact, Independent Sector (2001) found that people who regularly attended religious services volunteered at a much higher rate (54 percent) than those who did not attend services (32 percent).

Consider recruiting families as groups. Recent research by First Side Partners shows that people who volunteer alongside family members donate their time more regularly (45 percent) than those who do not volunteer with family members (33 percent). They also volunteer an average of 4.3 hours per week, compared to 2.8 hours for people who volunteer on their own.

Don't forget about the single folks in your community. Single people are often looking for ways to meet people—and volunteering is a great way to do just that. Single Volunteers, Inc., is devoted to promoting volunteerism among single people. You can find information about local chapters at *www.SingleVolunteers.org*.

■ **Target people who love animals.** Post brochures in veterinary offices, zoos, aquariums, pet supply stores, and dog-training facilities and be sure to put a call for volunteers in your organizational newsletter and fund-raising letters.

■ **Reach beyond the territory of animal lovers.** Don't assume that all do-gooders who walk through your doors are there because they love animals. They may have other motivations: perhaps they're lonely or new to the area and want to make friends. Michigan's Capital Area Humane Society provides realtors with welcome packets, including information about the humane society, with a list of volunteer opportunities and orientation dates, for community newcomers. Other potential volunteers may want to build skills in "animal-free" fields, such as newsletter production, or building maintenance.

■ **Consider volunteers with special needs.** Organizations that provide care for people with developmental disabilities often seek activities for their charges. Consider working with such groups to help your shelter with basic tasks.

■ **Recruit for diversity.** Try to involve all segments of your community in your volunteer program. Reach out to ethnic groups in your area and invite them to participate in your program.

■ **Appeal to responsible kids.** Involving children in your volunteer program requires special planning, but it can provide many benefits. For more information on children as volunteers, see chapter 8.

■ **Involve senior citizens.** People approaching retirement indicate that they plan to volunteer once they do retire.

A survey of older Americans (aged 50–75) by Peter D. Hart Research Associates (2002) found that more than half (56 percent) of seniors say that civic engagement will be at least a fairly important part of retirement:

> Three in five (59 percent) older Americans...say that, from their point of view, retirement is "a time to be active and involved, to start new activities, and to set new goals." Just a quarter (24 percent) of all older adults and 16 percent of older adult volunteers say that retirement is a time to enjoy leisure activities and take a much-deserved rest. (4)

A web site is dedicated to helping seniors find volunteer work in their community. Check out *www.seniorcorps.org* for more information.

Figure 3
Volunteers by Age, by Percentage

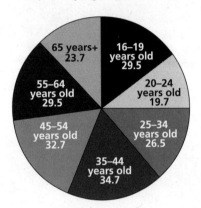

35–44 year olds were the most likely to volunteer; followed closely by 45–54 year olds. Be sure to target these age groups in your volunteer recruitment efforts.

Source: United States Department of Labor, Bureau of Labor Statistics 2003.

The Role of a Community Volunteer Center

If you are lucky enough to have a volunteer center in your community, take advantage of its services. It can help you find the perfect volunteer for the position you need filled, including specialized or skilled positions such as photographers or artists. It can also redirect volunteers you don't need to positions within other organizations. Beyond assisting with recruitment, such a center often can provide guidance on developing your volunteer program and may even offer training to help you and your staff work better with volunteers. Volunteer centers generally just make your job easier!

The Points of Light Foundation and Volunteer Center National Network offer an online searchable database of volunteer centers across the country. To search for the volunteer center nearest you, visit *www.pointsoflight.org/centers/find_center.cfm*.

Staff as Volunteers

What do you do if staff members also want to volunteer for the organization? For example, an administrative staff member who handles the front reception area decides she wants to foster a litter of puppies as a volunteer. How should this be handled?

To avoid any potential employment-related labor disputes down the road, you should consult your attorney or municipal human resources department. The volunteer work should be different from that in the employee's paid position, and the work should be done outside of normal working hours. Treat staff volunteers as you treat other volunteers: staff volunteers should complete applications, attend volunteer orientation, receive training, and track their volunteer hours. Document the relationship in case a question or dispute arises about the individual's employment status.

Should a staff member's relative be allowed to volunteer? Yes, but assign staff and close family or friends different tasks in different areas of the facility. This policy will help you avoid the appearance of conflict of interest or favoritism.

Figure 4

How Volunteers Became Involved with their Volunteer Organization, by Percentage

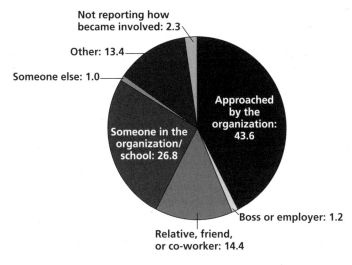

Not reporting how became involved: 2.3

Other: 13.4

Someone else: 1.0

Someone in the organization/school: 26.8

Approached by the organization: 43.6

Boss or employer: 1.2

Relative, friend, or co-worker: 14.4

The most common way volunteers became involved with their volunteer organization was by being approached directly by that organization. By directly asking people to volunteer for your organization, you are greatly increasing the likelihood that they will participate rather than waiting for them to decide to seek out your cause on their own.

Source: U.S. Department of Labor, Bureau of Labor Statistics 2003.

Board Members as Volunteers

Members of the board of directors of newly formed or all-volunteer humane organizations are often involved in just about everything from cleaning kennels and providing direct animal care to writing brochures and counseling the public about responsible pet ownership. As the organization matures and recruits an executive director, employees, and nonboard volunteers, the board of directors should begin to back out of the organization's day-to-day operations.

In a well-established and healthy organization, the board's role should be to govern, not manage. Too many humane society boards spend too much of their time on operational issues such as determining cage-cleaning schedules or interfering with staffing decisions. With the exception of organizations that are new, very small, or run completely by volunteers (where board members *are* the staff), humane societies should discourage their boards from discussing such administrative details. Those concerns should be left in the hands of the staff hired by the board. The board's responsibility is to focus on the big-picture issues such as organizational mission and policy. Although the board is accountable for the means, its primary focus must be on the ends.

While the role of board members is much different from that of other volunteers, they are still volunteers. They need to understand their role and know what is expected of them. These expectations should be laid out clearly in writing as part of a board manual and updated regularly. Board members should have written job descriptions outlining their role on the board of directors, just as other volunteers do at the shelter. Board orientations should be developed so that newly appointed board members understand how they fit into the overall picture.

It is not uncommon for board members to be involved with special events or fund-raising efforts, since a big part of their role is maintaining the financial health of the organization. However, proceed carefully if a board member wants to be actively involved in adoptions, dog training, cat socializing, or other day-to-day activities. Without adequate structure, the fragile relationship between staff and board can easily become confused or damaged when board members work in operations and are supervised by staff. It is hard for both staff members and board members to remember that one board member has no individual authority—authority comes from the board of directors as a whole.

Some organizations do encourage board members to come to the shelter and help out with hands-on activities. They feel such exposure to staff experiences helps the board to be sympathetic to the problems and challenges staff members face. Without such involvement, the thinking goes, the board of directors sometimes comes up with some very unrealistic ideas about how things should be done.

If your organization decides to allow board members to volunteer for other jobs, establish clear ground rules. A board member who wants to volunteer at the shelter—grooming dogs, for example—should first be required to temporarily replace his or her "board hat" with a "volunteer hat." The individual must act—and expect to be treated—as any other volunteer supervised by staff rather than as a member of the board who governs the organization. Board members also must go through the same orientation and training process as do all other shelter volunteers.

If this arrangement creates tension among staff or interferes with operations overseen by the executive director—for example, if a board member volunteering in the adoption ward bypasses channels to challenge an adoption or euthanasia decision—your organization should reconsider its policy of allowing board members to volunteer in the shelter alongside staff. A board member who prefers nonboard volunteer activities, such as socializing cats or helping adopters, should resign his or her board position. This decision prevents conflict of interest and enables the individual to focus on the jobs he or she truly enjoys.

For assistance with general board development, see the volunteer-management-related web sites listed on page 109.

Special Issues for Government Agencies

Using volunteers can be a sensitive topic for government agencies that have employee unions. However, active volunteer programs expand citizen understanding of, involvement in, and support for animal services programs. They often inspire creativity and improve staff morale. The concerns of organized labor over potential loss of paid staff positions to volunteer labor have been addressed successfully in public animal care organizations throughout the United States—including at the Seattle (Washington) Animal Shelter and Fort Wayne (Indiana) Animal Care and Control. In these organizations, volunteers work in tandem with paid employees, taking on tasks that supplement but fall outside of staff responsibilities, thus making staff jobs easier and/or more rewarding.

Generally speaking, in union situations, volunteers can't do everything the staff is paid to do. If staff members are paid to clean the shelter, for example, volunteers cannot come in just to clean. That may not mean, however, that volunteers can't periodically scoop animal waste throughout the day as needed. As long as you don't allow volunteers to take over critical tasks, the program should run smoothly. Just be sure that you adhere to the union contract and that the union understands that volunteers will supplement, not substitute for, staff jobs.

Many municipal agencies have helped create separate "Friends of the Animal Shelter" groups. The groups are nonprofit organizations formed solely to support the local municipal shelter. The arrangement requires a big commitment on the part of the volunteers, who have to go through the intensive process of incorporating as a nonprofit. However, such arrangements allow government agencies to benefit from volunteer help and fund raising while avoiding the hassles of incorporating volunteers into a public agency. This kind of setup is not unique to animal care and control. In fact, most communities have volunteer groups such as the "Friends of the Public Library" or the "Friends of the Park."

Developing an agreement with the labor union or establishing a "friends of" group can be a great way for a municipal agency to take advantage of volunteer assistance. Just make sure the program is carefully structured to avoid a situation where volunteers feel they can run the show.

Should You Accept Court-Ordered Community Service Volunteers?

Court-ordered volunteers are required to perform their volunteer service because they have broken the law. That doesn't mean these individuals won't make good volunteers. Just know that such a program requires special consideration and should not be accepted lightly. Before bringing in court-ordered volunteers, take time to think through the following issues:

■ Who will oversee the program? Will it be the volunteer coordinator, or should a staff manager handle court-ordered volunteers because they require extra supervision?

■ Which offenders will be permitted? Most animal shelters will not accept animal abusers, violent criminals, or drug violators. Your organization will have to tell the courts what the shelter is comfortable accepting.

■ Will the court-ordered program be integrated into the general volunteer program? If so, how will this be handled? Court-ordered volunteers should not be offered the same benefits as other volunteers are and, in most cases, will need well-defined tasks that do not involve animal handling.

■ How will you deal with the additional liability operating such a program entails? For example, how will you ensure proper supervision to ensure safety for the staff, volunteers, and animals the offender may come into contact with?

Don't participate in a court-ordered program until your regular volunteer program is running smoothly, but don't rule out the idea indefinitely. Although court-ordered programs require careful planning, they can also provide a good opportunity to have your chain-link fence in the kennels repaired or fresh paint applied to the walls of your education room.

Conducting a Volunteer Orientation

As part of the recruitment process, you'll want to invite potential volunteers to an orientation, which provides an opportunity for volunteers to see who you are and what you do before they decide whether your organization is right for them. Be open about what you're proud of and what you hope to improve. And be clear and positive throughout: remember, even those who decide not to volunteer can spread the word about your work. If they like what they see, you'll like what they say.

Here are some tips to help you create a winning orientation:

■ **Survey current staff and volunteers,** if you have them, to learn what they wish they'd known when they started working for your organization. Provide a written questionnaire or just sit down with some of your volunteers and ask them: What do you wish someone had told you about volunteering here before you started? What was confusing for you? What advice would you give a new volunteer? Find out who's been the best guide and source of information for volunteers since they arrived at your organization. Getting feedback from current volunteers will help you create a comprehensive and helpful orientation, and it will give your volunteers the satisfaction of knowing you're interested in what they have to say.

■ **Write a script.** Create a written outline of what you will cover during the orientation and have the staff review it and offer comments. Having a written plan will also allow others to fill in for you if you cannot make it to an orientation.

■ **Include a variety of speakers.** It's important that the audience hear an array of voices, not just the volunteer coordinator's. Invite key staff and volunteers to give brief overviews of their jobs. Try to include the people with whom volunteers will have the most interaction, such as your adoption counselor, kennel worker, euthanasia technician, and veterinarian. Ask a seasoned volunteer to speak to the group about his or her experience at the organization. Potential volunteers are more likely to join you if your representatives show enthusiasm about their jobs and the shelter. You can even bring in outside voices: *Power of Compassion* is a good introductory video about the world of shelter work; available to shelters at a discount through Pyramid Media (*www.pyramidmedia.com*), it can help give your audience a glimpse of how your organization fits into the bigger picture.

■ **Make visitors comfortable.** When potential volunteers arrive, have them congregate in a cheerful, relatively quiet area away from the hustle and bustle of staff and visitors. Consider providing light refreshments.

■ **Explain who you are.** Provide a good introduction to what your organization does, how you got started, and what programs have gotten you where you are today. Explain the services you provide and how volunteers are critical in making them possible; also explain your goals for the future and how volunteers can help you reach them.

■ **Discuss sensitive topics.** For example, explain how euthanasia is performed and how euthanasia decisions are made. Also discuss stressful situations volunteers may face when working in the shelter—distraught owners looking for their lost pets, abused animals, and angry or disappointed potential adopters who have been rejected. Help volunteers understand how decisions are made and who makes them. Invite them to direct questions to designated staff but emphasize that volunteers are expected to support the staff, not challenge existing policy.

■ **Talk about the benefits of volunteering.** You can energize potential volunteers by talking about the happy side of working in the shelter: helping create lifelong relationships and caring for homeless animals are experiences you can't get anywhere else.

■ **Give a tour of the shelter.** Explain the functions of all areas of the facility and relate them to your organization's larger goals and mission. Show them where volunteers store their belongings during their shifts, where they sign in, where supplies are stored, and other logistical details. Point out areas that may be off-limits to volunteers, such as the euthanasia room and quarantine areas, and explain why those areas are for staff only.

■ **Send them home wanting more.** After the tour, allow time for questions, then thank attendees for their time. Distribute written information for them to take home and review. Request any paperwork you might need from them, too—this is a great time to invite interested attendees to complete an application to get the ball rolling. Make sure potential volunteers understand the next steps: do they need to call you for a phone interview or should they set up an in-person appointment? Have your schedule handy so you can book times for interviews or training sessions for those who are ready to commit.

For best results, try to vary your orientation times. If you want to promote diversity and involve a variety of volunteers, you'll need to be flexible. Consider alternating evenings and weekends for orientations to accommodate as many potentially interested volunteers as possible. Review the times you're actually going to need volunteers to work and hold orientations during those shifts.

If you plan things well, you'll probably get a great new crew of helpers. Even if you don't, a volunteer orientation is not only an opportunity to recruit volunteers but also an educational experience for those who attend. Some of the people who attend may never come back, but they should come away empowered to help animals in other ways—whether through adopting their next pet or sterilizing the animals already in their households. A good orientation will give attendees a greater understanding and appreciation of the role of your organization in the community.

SPCA
Serving Erie County

Welcome to the Erie County SPCA

Thank you for showing an interest in volunteering here at the shelter.

SPCA Volunteer Orientation Instructions & Agenda

Upon arrival: Please help yourself to refreshments and be seated. You will have a chance to take program literature and fill out forms later. While seated please read over the "SPCA volunteer programs packet." Please pay close attention to the experience required and the days and times we need your help.

1) **Intro:** SPCA background & services—Kim Zolnowski (Volunteer Coordinator)

2) **Video:** *The Power of Compassion*—How animal shelters evolved, what we do as an SPCA, etc.

3) **Tour of the Shelter:** (SPCA volunteers & Volunteer Coordinator)

4) **Review:** the volunteer opportunities that you are interested in.

5) **Completion of application:** ***Application Procedures***
   a. Please be sure to fill out in order of preference what volunteer jobs you would be interested in and also days and times available.
   b. It is especially important to list any physical or mental conditions you have in case we need to modify a job program to meet your health needs.
   c. List all your program choices in order of preference, even if there are not any openings in that department at this time. You will be called as soon as an opening occurs for the days and times you are available.
   d. You will only be required to work one specific day and time per week for high-commitment-level programs, unless otherwise stated. I need to know all the possible days and times you could work in each department. If one shift fills up quickly, we have others to choose from.

PLEASE NOTE: Job description packets are limited.
Please take only those that you are seriously considering.

After the Orientation

After reviewing all applications, I will be contacting volunteers by department for an interview based on your choices, availability and related job experience. **It may take up to 3 months before I have completed contacting and training some applicants.**

Chapter 5

Screening Volunteers

Volunteer Applications

The purpose of a volunteer application is to help you establish the applicant's skills and interests so you can determine whether the individual will be a good fit for the organization. Think carefully about what information you need from the person applying. You will need to match prospective volunteers with appropriate positions within your organization, so ask them to list not only general contact information but also occupations, special skills and hobbies, availability, previous volunteer experiences, and experience with animals. The more you know about an applicant, the better match you can make. However, don't inundate applicants with questions; sometimes the simpler you keep the application the better.

Consider requesting the following information when creating your shelter's application:

- Name, address, home and work phone numbers
- E-mail address
- Date of birth
- Driver's license number
- Emergency contact information
- Occupation
- Special skills and hobbies (such as fluency in a foreign language)
- Previous volunteer experience
- Experience with animals
- Education level
- Times and days available to volunteer
- Here is a list of volunteer positions...Please indicate areas of interest.
- Are there any duties you would prefer *not* to do?
- Personal or work references
- Any allergies, physical disabilities, or other limitations that may require accommodation or may restrict volunteer experience
- How did you hear about our volunteer program?
- Are you a member of our organization?
- Do you have pets at home? What kind? Are they spayed or neutered?
- Why do you want to volunteer for our organization?

The following pages contain a few sample volunteer applications that will help you in developing or improving your own.

Iowa City/Coralville Animal Care and Adoption Center

Volunteer Application

Last Name _____ **First Name** _____ Nickname _____

Address _____

Day Phone _____ Evening Phone _____

E-mail _____ Date of Birth _____

EMERGENCY Contact & Relationship _____ **Phone** _____

Why are you interested in becoming a volunteer at our Center? _____

Describe any previous experience working with animals: _____

_____

List present and previous volunteer jobs: _____

_____

Occupation and Employer: _____

_____

May we call you at work? _____ If yes, phone # _____

Educational experience (if currently in school, include name of school, grade and course of study):

_____

List additional information that may be useful (i.e., special skills, training, interests, hobbies): ____

_____

Please check days and times you prefer:

Shift Times	Monday	Tuesday	Wednesday	Thursday	Friday	Saturday	Sunday
6:30–9:00 a.m.							
9:00 a.m.–12:00 p.m.							
12:00–3:00 p.m.							
3:00–6:00 p.m.							

I give my permission to the Iowa City/Coralville Animal Care and Adoption Center to verify the above information. I understand that this application does not guarantee acceptance to the ICCACAC volunteer program.

_____ _____
Volunteer Signature and Date   Parent/Guardian Signature/Date (if volunteer is under 18)

continued…

Areas of Volunteer Interest

Please let us know what your current and future interests are.

Dog and Cat training not required for the following areas. Special training will be provided.

- ❑ Clerical
- ❑ Community Events
- ❑ Greeter
- ❑ Facility Building and Grounds
- ❑ Featured Pet Poster Preparation
- ❑ Kong Preparation

After completing Green Level Cat or Dog Training:

- ❑ Cat Volunteer
- ❑ Communications Folder Maintenance
- ❑ Dog Volunteer
- ❑ Foster Care (some animals may require Yellow or Red Dog training)
- ❑ Humane Education Volunteer
- ❑ Kennel Assistant
- ❑ Lost and Found Folder Maintenance
- ❑ Rescue Transport (some animals may require Yellow or Red Dog training)

After completing Red Level Cat or Dog Training:

- ❑ Adoption Counselor
- ❑ Dog Trainer (Red Dog only)
- ❑ Instructor for Volunteer Training
- ❑ Mentor

Champaign County Humane Society
1911 E. Main Street
Urbana, IL 61802
Phone: 217-344-9314
Fax 217-344-7299
www.cuhumane.org

Date Submitted _____

VOLUNTEER APPLICATION

Please provide your personal information:
(Personal information is for CCHS use only)

Name_____ Age _____

Address_____ Apt _____

City, State, Zip _____

Home Phone _____

E-mail address _____

Please choose your area(s) of interest from the following list:
Mark the areas you are most interested in with numbered ranking.

___ Dog walking   ___ Ph.D. (training)   ___ Petsmart
___ Cat socializing   ___ Fostering   ___ Grooming
___ Cage cleaning   ___ Events   ___ Other (please specify)
___ Medical assistant

Please provide a contact person in case of emergency:

Emergency contact _____

Relationship _____

Home phone_____

Alternate phone _____

Please list the days and times that you are most likely to volunteer:

_____

_____

List any volunteer groups you are involved with (RSVP, VIP, etc.):

_____

_____

Please provide any additional skills you may have that will assist us in finding specialized positions for you in our volunteer program:

_____

_____

Have you volunteered with our organization in the past? If so, when?

_____

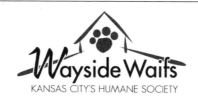

Wayside Waifs
KANSAS CITY'S HUMANE SOCIETY

THANK YOU for your interest in volunteering with Wayside Waifs! Tails are wagging and cats are meowing in excitement over your participation! Volunteers play a vital role within our organization. Without your support, we would not be able to assist nearly the number of animals who need help in our community.

Please complete the Adult Volunteer Application below (you must be over 18 years of age to participate in the adult volunteer program). Select the volunteer activities that most interest you. Upon receipt of your application, I will notify you of the dates for our next Volunteer Orientation. Specifics about each volunteer activity will be discussed further in the orientation meeting. Depending on the activities you choose, additional training may be required. **Please print your responses clearly**. Thank you again for your interest in Wayside Waifs!

Date _____

Last Name _____ First Name _____ MI _____
Address _____
City _____ State _____ Zip _____
Home Phone _____ Work Phone _____
Alt. Phone _____ E-mail Address _____ Date of Birth _____
Emergency Contact _____ Relation _____
Contact Phone _____ Alt. Phone _____

Education:

Are you currently enrolled in high school or college? ❑ no ❑ yes
If yes, what is the name of your school? _____

(Circle last year completed)
High School   1 2 3 4   College   1 2 3 4   Graduate   1 2 3 4

How did you hear about the volunteer program at Wayside Waifs? _____
_____
_____

Do you have experience working with animals? ❑ no ❑ yes – please describe:_____
_____
_____

Describe any present or previous volunteer work you have done: _____
_____
_____

continued…

Do you have pets? ❑ no ❑ yes   Are they spayed or neutered? ❑ no ❑ yes
If no, have you or do you plan to breed them? ❑ no ❑ yes
Are you presently employed? ❑ no ❑ yes — may we contact you at work ❑ no ❑ yes

Employer:

_____

Describe the type of work you do: _____

_____

List any special skills, training, or hobbies: _____

_____

_____

Please check the volunteer opportunities you would like to participate in:

❑ Groomer   ❑ WAGS Trainer   ❑ Humane Educator
❑ Receptionist   ❑ Yard Work   ❑ Behavior Helpline
❑ Kennel Guide   ❑ Photography   ❑ PR/Special Events
❑ Cat Socializer   ❑ Mobile Adoptions   ❑ Adoption Counselor
❑ Dog Socializer   ❑ Computer Wizard   ❑ Foster Parent
❑ WeeWAGS Trainer   ❑ Speakers Bureau   ❑ Fundraising

Please check the animals you are comfortable handling and working with:

❑ Small/Med Dogs   ❑ Med/Large Dogs   ❑ Puppies   ❑ Cats   ❑ Kittens
❑ Rabbits, Guinea Pigs, or other small animals
List any other areas of interest not listed above: _____

Please indicate the time(s) you are available to volunteer:

Monday _____ Tuesday _____ Wednesday _____
Thursday_____ Friday _____ Saturday _____
Sunday _____ Anytime _____

Many times we need help transporting animals to and from special events, mobile adoption
fairs, etc. Please answer the following questions, keeping in mind your responses will be held
in the strictest confidence by Wayside Waifs Humane Society.

• Do you have a valid Missouri driver's license? ❑ no ❑ yes
• Do you have a valid Kansas driver's license? ❑ no ❑ yes
• Do you have your own transportation? ❑ no ❑ yes

continued…

Would you be willing to transport animals as part of your volunteer work?   ❏ no   ❏ yes
• If yes, is the car you would be driving covered by liability insurance?   ❏ no   ❏ yes
  • Name of Insurance Company_____
  • Have you ever pled guilty to a traffic violation?   ❏ no   ❏ yes
  • Excluding traffic violations, have you ever been convicted of any criminal offense?
     ❏ no   ❏ yes please explain: _____
Did a current volunteer recommend you volunteer at Wayside?   ❏ no   ❏ yes
If yes, please list their name so we may thank them   _____
Is there anyone you could suggest we call about volunteering at Wayside Waifs?   _____

_____

We would be very interested in any further information, comments, or questions you may have

_____

_____

I give permission to Wayside Waifs Humane Society to verify any information given above.

_____
Volunteer Signature   Date

Please return this application to:
Wayside Waifs Humane Society
Attn: Volunteer Coordinator
PO Box 9791
Kansas City, MO 64134-0791
Phone: (816) 761-8151
Fax: (816) 765-6888

**"From what we get, we can make a living;
what we give, however, makes a life."**
— *Arthur Ashe*

 **VOLUNTEER APPLICATION**

The Dumb Friends League encourages the participation of volunteers who support the following mission: "to provide shelter and care for animals; to provide programs and services which enhance the bond between animals and people; to be advocates for animals...speaking for those who cannot speak for themselves."

All potential volunteers must receive an interview prior to placement. We also require that all volunteers participate in our training program as part of their work experience. If you agree with our mission and are willing to be interviewed and trained, we encourage you to complete this application. The information on this form will help us to find the most satisfying and appropriate job for you. Please print your responses.

DATE: _____

NAME _____
       Title   First   Middle   Last   Nickname

MY BIRTH DATE IS _____
                (Month)   (Day)   (Year)

ADDRESS _____
                        City   Zip

HOME PHONE# _____ **WORK PHONE#** _____ **CELL #** _____

EMERGENCY# _____ **NAME** _____ **RELATIONSHIP** _____

E-MAIL _____

EDUCATION: (Circle last year completed)   **HIGH SCHOOL** 1 2 3 4
            COLLEGE 1 2 3 4   **GRADUATE** 1 2 3 4

NAME OF SCHOOL/COLLEGE _____

ARE YOU PRESENTLY EMPLOYED?   YES_____   NO_____

IF YES, STATE YOUR WORK SCHEDULE _____

EMPLOYER'S NAME AND ADDRESS _____

_____

INDUSTRY_____**POSITION**_____**PROFESSION**_____

-over-

continued…

PREVIOUS WORK EXPERIENCE _____

_____

SPECIAL SKILLS, TRAINING, INTERESTS, OR HOBBIES _____

_____

WHAT KIND OF VOLUNTEER JOB ARE YOU CURRENTLY INTERESTED IN? _____

_____

ARE YOU AVAILABLE REGULARLY EACH WEEK? YES_____ NO _____

PLEASE INDICATE THE TIME WHICH YOU WOULD BE AVAILABLE FOR WORK:

MONDAY_____ **FRIDAY**_____

TUESDAY_____ **SATURDAY** _____

WEDNESDAY_____ **SUNDAY** _____

THURSDAY_____ **ALMOST ANY TIME**_____

As a benefit, the League provides, through a special policy, excess auto and accident insurance to all our volunteers during the course of their volunteer duties. In this regard, please answer the following questions keeping in mind that your responses will be held in the strictest confidence by the DFL.

DO YOU HAVE A VALID COLORADO DRIVER'S LICENSE? YES_____ NO _____

DO YOU HAVE A CAR AND WOULD YOU BE WILLING TO DRIVE IT TO TRANSPORT ANIMALS AS PART OF YOUR VOLUNTEER WORK? YES_____ NO _____

IF YES, IS THE CAR YOU WOULD BE DRIVING COVERED BY LIABILITY INSURANCE?
YES_____ NO_____

HAVE YOU EVER PLED GUILTY TO A TRAFFIC VIOLATION? YES_____ NO_____

IF YES, PLEASE EXPLAIN_____

_____

_____

EXCLUDING A TRAFFIC VIOLATION, HAVE YOU EVER BEEN CONVICTED OF ANY CRIMINAL OFFENSE? YES_____ NO_____ IF YES, PLEASE EXPLAIN _____

continued…

HOW DID YOU HEAR ABOUT THE DFL VOLUNTEER PROGRAM? _____

_____

WHY ARE YOU INTERESTED IN BECOMING A DFL VOLUNTEER? _____

_____

DESCRIBE ANY PREVIOUS EXPERIENCE WORKING WITH ANIMALS _____

_____

DESCRIBE PRESENT AND PREVIOUS VOLUNTEER JOBS _____

_____

**WE WOULD BE INTERESTED IN ANY FURTHER INFORMATION YOU MIGHT
WISH TO OFFER** _____

PLEASE LIST TWO (2) REFERENCES, WHO ARE NOT FAMILY MEMBERS:

_____
NAME   RELATIONSHIP   PHONE NUMBER

_____
NAME   RELATIONSHIP   PHONE NUMBER

I give my permission to the DFL to verify any of the information given.

_____
                                            (Volunteer Signature)

- -

DEPARTMENT USE: NEW VOLUNTEER INFORMATION

                                            Specific Dept. Trng.

VOLUNTEER'S NAME _____

Interview Date _____   Placement _____   DATE _____

Training Date _____   Shift _____   TIME _____

Interviewer _____   Start Date _____   TRAINER _____

Interviewing Potential Volunteers

It makes perfect sense to interview job applicants, but why interview volunteers? Interviewing prospective volunteers can help you prevent a bad match, saving you time and frustration in the end. Conducting interviews with volunteers shows them that you take your program seriously and want to give them a job that's right for them.

Since time is always a limiting factor, you may choose not to conduct a one-on-one interview for every volunteer position. Many organizations base this decision on the position level. For example, an entry-level position for dog walking may not call for an interview. However, it's best to interview volunteers who will be doing adoption counseling to ensure they have the necessary skills to handle such a sensitive position.

Here's some advice to help you make the most of your interviews:

- **Hold the interview in a quiet place free from interruptions.** Take the interview seriously—don't answer the phone or perform other tasks while conducting an interview. Such interruptions prevent you from getting to know the volunteer and may make the individual uncomfortable. Although the interview doesn't have to be long, allow enough time to explore an applicant's interests, experience, and needs so you can best match prospective volunteers with the right positions.

- **Create a list of questions to ask during the interview.** Having a written list will help keep you on track and make sure you treat all potential volunteers equally. Open-ended questions work well and can be very revealing. Ask a prospective volunteer what he or she would do if an upset citizen confronted him or her about being denied an adoption. You can also ask the individual to share his or her views on neutering and euthanasia. Tailor your questions to the positions. For example, if you are recruiting dog walkers, ask them to describe how they would handle a shy or scared dog.

- **Pay attention to the applicant's skills.** Is the individual a good speaker? Does the individual have fund-raising experience? Is the individual fluent in Spanish? Consider how these skills can help your organization achieve its mission and enable volunteers to put their talents to good use.

- **Clarify both the organization's and the applicant's expectations.** Review the job description with the prospective volunteer and talk about the various aspects of what's expected and what is or is not permitted. Ask the applicant if he or she is comfortable performing the tasks listed in the job description.

■ **Allow time for questions and concerns.** Tell applicants up front about any unappealing aspects of the job. If these are explained well, volunteers will usually be agreeable. If you're not honest with them, however, they may grow disillusioned and leave. Be prepared to answer questions about your organization's position on difficult issues.

At the end of the interview, make sure the applicant knows what will happen next. Should the individual wait to hear from you about whether he or she has been accepted? If you've accepted the individual on the spot, when should he or she start? How will training be scheduled? The Dumb Friends League created the friendly "New Volunteer Reminder" form on the next page to help fresh volunteers wade through the process.

New Volunteer Reminder

**Thank you for choosing the Dumb Friends League to volunteer!
We welcome you to our organization!**

Below are the dates and times you need to mark your calendar:

Training Date: _____

Training Time: 9:00 a.m. – 3:00 p.m.

in the Education Center on the south side of the Quebec Street shelter.

Specific Department Training Date: _____

Specific Department Training Time: _____

Trainer's Name: _____

Please meet your trainer _____

First Shift Date: _____

First Shift Time: _____

☐ Report directly to your supervisor in _____

   Supervisor's Name: _____

☐ Please come to the general offices upstairs and we will get you started.

_____

_____

If you have any questions or problems, please call 303-696-4941
ext. 7246 for Jodi Schulz or ext. 7247 for Mary Dechant.

Thank you!

The staff and the animals will be glad to see you!

p/volunteer/volreminder 11/04/04

To Check or Not to Check?

Whether you conduct reference or background checks—and to what extent—will vary, depending on the volunteer positions you offer and your agency's policies. Calling organizations the person has volunteered for, contacting his or her current employer, or checking driving or criminal records can be helpful. But it can also be time-consuming, so choose carefully what you decide to check.

Formal criminal background checks can be expensive and are usually not necessary for most animal shelter volunteer programs. The laws related to background checks vary from state to state, so if your organization is considering such a procedure, be sure to find out what your state's requirements and limitations are before proceeding. Also keep in mind that background checks are usually done only in the state in which the person currently lives; they may not give you historical information from previous states of residence.

Before implementing any background check system, be sure parameters are set in a written policy statement explaining how the information obtained will be used. What level of offense would preclude a prospective volunteer from joining your organization? If someone was charged with trespassing at the age of eighteen, would you ban that individual from your program? What if a background check revealed assault and burglary charges? Which offenses are acceptable and which ones raise a red flag? Creating clear guidelines now will ensure that all prospective volunteers are treated equally and without discrimination.

Conducting background or reference checks brings with it greater responsibility for the volunteer manager. It is crucial that the information obtained in the background check be kept confidential. This information should not be shared with other staff and volunteers. It should be placed inside a locked filing cabinet and given the same care accorded to staff personnel files. Electronic files should be password-protected, and only key management staff should have access to them.

If you do perform reference or background checks, you should first get written permission from the prospective volunteer. If you check driving records, need proof of insurance, or run background checks of criminal records through the police department, you'll want to create a simple permission form that prospective volunteers sign. Your best bet is to check work references or references from previous volunteer jobs, then practice good risk management (see chapter 9). If you do that, you may be able to skip the formal criminal background check altogether. Discuss your options with your organization's attorney and have him or her review any forms you ask volunteers to sign.

Saying, "No Thanks!"

During the recruitment process, the organization should look for energetic individuals with specific goals and talents. Because of people's overwhelming interest in animals, some animal care organizations and their volunteer coordinators come to believe that the shelter is there for the volunteers rather than the other way around. Be careful not to make that mistake. Only accept those volunteers who can meet your needs and whose needs you can meet in return. Always remember that it's better to have just a few good volunteers than a number of mediocre ones. Your shelter is not obligated to find opportunities for every willing volunteer, but it does need to find a willing and suitable volunteer for every job you need done.

If you're not comfortable saying no in the face-to-face interview, you can always follow up with a letter or e-mail. Take a look at this sample letter used by the Dumb Friends League:

Jane Doe
123 Main Street
Denver, CO 80231

Re: Volunteer Opportunities

Dear Jane,

Thank you very much for submitting a volunteer application. We appreciate your considering volunteering at the Dumb Friends League.

Unfortunately at this time, we don't have a position available for you. We will, however, keep your application on file for 60 days and will contact you if we are able to place you within that time.

Again, thank you for your interest in the Dumb Friends League's volunteer program.

Sincerely,

Jodi Schulz

Jodi L. Schulz
Volunteer Services Manager

The Volunteer Agreement

Many shelters use a volunteer agreement that sets forth the responsibilities of volunteers and your organization. It confirms with the volunteer what is expected and can be a helpful tool for letting volunteers go, when necessary. It can be part of the application, but it may be more effective as a stand-alone document that is signed once the person is accepted as a volunteer.

Keep the agreement simple and clear. Include a statement asserting that volunteers understand and agree to support the organization's mission and policies. A copy of the signed agreement should be given to the volunteer, and the original should be filed in the volunteer's file.

The following volunteer agreements can help you develop your own. Of course, be sure to have your organization's attorney review any documents you develop that you will ask volunteers to sign.

**City of Seattle
Department of Executive Administration
Seattle Animal Shelter**

SERVICE AGREEMENT FOR REGISTERED VOLUNTEERS

The City of Seattle, acting by and through its Department of Executive Administration (called the "Department" herein), and _____ (called the "Volunteer" herein), agree as follows:

1. The Department shall:
    a. Provide the Volunteer with such training, supervision, staff support, work space, uniforms and materials as the Department deems necessary to enable the Volunteer to perform his/her donated support services;
    b. Provide the Volunteer insurance for an on-the-job injury and personal injury and property damage liability insurance coverage (limit of $1,000,000 per occurrence, $25,000 per occurrence for medical) at no cost to the Volunteer for any claims arising out of the Volunteer's service as a registered Volunteer. This coverage shall not apply to the Volunteer's use of automobiles;
    c. Provide Volunteer with authorization to drive a City vehicle when required to do so in performing official City business at the request of Department and provide liability insurance coverage in the amount of $500,000 per occurrence, in excess of the Volunteer's personal auto liability insurance coverage, which shall be in force only during such times that the Volunteer is acting in a bona fide capacity, subject to proof of a valid Washington State Driver's License and proof of personal auto liability insurance coverage. In the event a claim or legal action arises out of an accident involving Volunteer's authorized use of a City vehicle, the Department will request such action be defended by the City's Corporation Counsel, in accordance with provision of Seattle Municipal Code 4.68.030.

2. The Volunteer shall:
    a. Provide a minimum of eight (8) hours per month for six (6) months performing volunteer service;
    b. Abide by and conform to Department and City policies relative to appearance, discipline, attendance, caliber of work, and written and oral directives;
    c. Be personally responsible for prompt and accurate recording of his/her hours of actual work on forms provided by the Department;
    d. Notify the Department when circumstances dictate termination of his/her volunteer service if prior to the date agreed upon in Section 3;
    e. Indemnify and hold the City of Seattle free and harmless from all liability arising out of any and all claims, demands, losses, damages, action, judgment of every kind and description which may occur to or be suffered by the Volunteer by reason of activities arising out of this agreement;
    f. Provide a copy of a current Washington State Driver's License and a copy of the personal auto liability insurance coverage prior to driving a City vehicle.

3. This agreement will be terminated upon ten (10) days' written or oral notice by either party to the other.

DATED THIS _____ DAY OF _____ 20 _____

VOLUNTEER NAME (print) _____

VOLUNTEER SIGNATURE _____

ADDRESS _____

HOME PHONE _____

VOLUNTEER PROJECT (if any) _____

LOCATION _____

VOLUNTEER PROGRAMS COORDINATOR _____

ARIZONA HUMANE SOCIETY
We Build Healthy Relationships Between People and Animals.

As a Volunteer with The Arizona Humane Society (AHS), I agree to:

- Never strike an animal, or handle or treat an animal in such a way that it would be construed as rough or abusive. I will always exercise compassion and care with the animals.
- Hold absolutely confidential all information that I may obtain, directly or indirectly, concerning clients, animals and staff. I agree not to seek to obtain confidential information from a client. I understand that an intentional or unintentional violation of confidentiality may result in disciplinary action, including termination by The Arizona Humane Society and/or possible legal action by others (i.e., clients, customers).
- Be available to volunteer for a minimum of 6 months and 50 hours.
- Become familiar with AHS policies and procedures, and uphold their philosophy and standards. I will seek clarification from a Volunteer Services representative, the Lead Docent or staff when required.
- Donate my services to The AHS without contemplation of compensation or future employment.
- Adhere to AHS policy of not taking pictures on AHS property, and not interfacing with members of the media unless otherwise instructed by AHS V.P. level personnel.
- Be punctual and conscientious, conduct myself with dignity, courtesy, and consideration for others, and strive to make my work professional in quality.
- Purchase and maintain appropriate Volunteer attire and maintain a well-groomed appearance for all Volunteer assignments.
- Attend supplemental and advanced training whenever possible.
- Carry out my assignments in accordance with AHS training, and seek assistance from a Volunteer Services representative, Lead Docent or AHS staff whenever necessary.
- Limit my activity to my assigned work area unless otherwise directed by a Volunteer Services representative, Lead Docent or AHS staff member.
- Communicate any job-related problems, concerns, differences of opinion, conflicts, or suggestions only to the Volunteer Services Manager or Lead Docent.
- Adhere to sign-in and scheduling procedures.
- Notify the Volunteer Services Department when I am unable to work as scheduled.
- Notify the Volunteer Services Department if I choose to discontinue my volunteer service with AHS.

I understand that The Arizona Humane Society reserves the right to terminate my Volunteer status as a result of any of the following:
- Any abuse or mistreatment of an animal.
- Failure to comply with organizational policies, rules, and other regulations.
- Unsatisfactory attitude, work, or appearance.
- Any other circumstances which, in the judgment of the Volunteer Services Manager and/or Volunteer Services Director, would make my continued service as a Volunteer contrary to the best interest of The Arizona Humane Society.

I have read and understand each of the above conditions. My signature below indicates that I agree to comply with them.

_____

Printed Name   Signature   Date

THE HUMANE SOCIETY OF THE UNITED STATES

Dallas Spay-Neuter and Animal Wellness Center

VOLUNTEER AGREEMENT

My name is _____ and I hereby agree to accept a position in a *voluntary* capacity as a *volunteer* for The Humane Society of the United States Spay-Neuter and Animal Wellness Center (hereinafter referred to as The HSUS). I understand that the term *voluntary* means the way in which actions or services are rendered to The HSUS. Such actions and services are rendered to The HSUS with generous and charitable motives. No liability whatsoever will be incurred by The HSUS to anyone who performs *voluntary* services. I understand that *volunteer* means a person who freely chooses to render services to The HSUS in a *voluntary* capacity.

Terms and Conditions

Please initial:

_____   I fully understand that my services are provided strictly in a voluntary capacity and I agree to provide my services to The HSUS strictly as a volunteer. I understand that I will receive no compensation, salary, employee benefits or payment of any kind for the services I render.

_____   I fully understand The HSUS clinic handles large numbers of animals on a daily basis. The temperament of these animals is often unknown to the HSUS clinic staff. I agree to hold The HSUS harmless for any injury(s) which I might sustain from handling animals during the course of my volunteer duties.

_____   I fully understand and agree to assume all risks involved in any and all duties that I perform for The HSUS in my volunteer capacity. Such duties might include, but are not limited to, animal handling, custodial work, kennel staff assistance and other volunteer duties.

_____   I agree to familiarize myself with HSUS policies and procedures and will fully comply with both the letter and spirit of these policies and procedures.

_____   I fully understand that The HSUS expects high standards of moral and ethical treatment of animals under its care. I agree to adhere strictly to these standards in my voluntary capacity at The HSUS.

_____   I agree not to represent The HSUS outside my immediate volunteer capacity. The HSUS employs designated spokesperson(s) to handle the concerns of animal welfare issues within and outside the Center.

_____   I fully understand and agree that either failure to comply with any and all of the obligations outlined in this Volunteer Agreement or for any reason whatsoever, while performing my volunteer services to The HSUS in a voluntary capacity, The HSUS, at its sole discretion, may immediately terminate my services.

 **VOLUNTEER AGREEMENT**

By signing below, I hereby accept a position as a Volunteer for the Dumb Friends League (the "League"), upon the following terms, conditions and understandings:

Terms and Conditions

1. My services to the League are provided strictly in a voluntary capacity as a Volunteer, and without any express or implied promise of salary, compensation or other payment of any kind whatsoever.
2. My services are furnished without any employment-type benefits, including employment insurance programs, worker's compensation accrual in any form, vacations or sick time.
3. I will familiarize myself and comply with the League's policies and procedures applicable to Volunteers. In particular, I fully understand that the League expects high standards of moral and ethical treatment of the animals under its care. I will adhere strictly to these standards in my capacity as a Volunteer.
4. I understand that the League, without notice or hearing, may terminate my services as a Volunteer at any time, with or without reason.

Release

1. I understand that the handling of animals and other Volunteer activities on behalf of the League may place me in a hazardous situation and could result in injury to me or my personal property. On behalf of myself, and my heirs, personal representatives and assigns, I hereby release, discharge, indemnify and hold harmless the League and its directors, officers, employees and agents from any and all claims, causes of action and demands of any nature, whether known or unknown, arising out of or in connection with my Volunteer activities on behalf of the League.
2. Understanding that public relations is an important part of a Volunteer's activities on behalf of the League, I hereby authorize the League to use any photographs of me in its possession for public relations purposes. I ask that the League use reasonable efforts to give me advance notice of any such use, but such notification is not a condition to release photographs for public relations purposes.

Date   Signature of Volunteer   Signature of Dumb Friends League
                                          Representative

If you are under 18, we must have your parent or legal guardian's signature below.

PARENT OR LEGAL GUARDIAN
(OF VOLUNTEERS 17 AND YOUNGER)

As a parent or legal guardian of the above-named Volunteer, I hereby give consent for my child or ward, as the case may be, to become a Volunteer for the Dumb Friends League as described in the above Volunteer Agreement and, by the signature below, join in and agree to be bound by the terms and conditions of the Release on the preceding page.

Date   Parent or Legal Guardian

Volunteers are the lifeblood of our organization. Whether your knack is stuffing envelopes, cuddling with the cats, grooming dogs, working on special projects, or walking the dogs, you are making a positive contribution and difference in the lives of the animals at the shelter.

As a volunteer representing Wayside, your conduct and interaction with staff, other volunteers and the public is expected to always be professional and courteous. In volunteering, you are making a commitment to staff and the animals to carry out, to the best of your abilities, the tasks you have pledged to perform.

The Volunteer Code of Ethics clarifies the expectations and principles for Wayside volunteers. Should a volunteer display unprofessional, dishonest or disrespectful behavior or exhibit a lack of self discipline, the volunteer will be asked to leave the premises. Such behavior could be grounds for termination of volunteer status.

Volunteer Code of Ethics
As a Wayside volunteer, I pledge to

Respect

- Respect others even though I may not agree with them
- Display courtesy, sensitivity, consideration and compassion for people and animals
- Use good judgment in recognizing the scope of authority of staff members

Safety

- Keep safety at the forefront of all volunteer activities
- Follow the rules presented to me in training
- Respect and use equipment and supplies as they are intended
- Report all injuries *immediately* to a staff person

Quality

- Perform all tasks to the best of my ability
- Ask for help when needed
- Recognize training is essential to maintain safe shelter practices

Self Discipline

- Recognize my limitations and those of others
- Set boundaries for myself—know my limits with the animals and other activities
- Hold myself accountable for the commitments I undertake

continued…

Communication

- Recognize I communicate both verbally and non-verbally
- Listen to the needs of others
- Advise shelter personnel of relevant information regarding the animals and my involvement at the shelter

Commitment

- Recognize true commitment comes from within
- Respect that people and animals count on me to honor my commitments
- Work together with staff and other volunteers to meet Wayside's goals

Welfare

- Value my role in the maintenance and growth of the organization
- Strive to promote a positive environment
- Respect and support all people and animals

_____

Volunteer Signature   Date

You have never really lived until you've done something
for someone who can never repay you.
                                          —*Unknown*

No act of kindness, however small, is ever wasted.
                                          —*Aesop*

Chapter 6

Training Volunteers

After they've been screened and accepted into the volunteer program, all volunteers should receive training before starting work. The goal of any good training program is to help volunteers perform their jobs well, confidently, and independently, without having to constantly interrupt the staff to ask questions. Make sure you provide volunteers with the knowledge and the tools required to complete tasks on their own.

The level of training provided will likely depend on the complexity of the positions. The more responsibility a volunteer has, the more training and supervision the individual requires. Untrained volunteers are less productive, demand more staff assistance, and make more mistakes, costing you much more time in the long run. You've taken the time to properly screen and orient volunteers, so don't drop the ball now!

Investing in a training program provides benefits over and above productive volunteers: some organizations say that their well-trained volunteers have more experience than do newly hired staff and can serve as mentors to them. And the training you develop for volunteers can be "recycled" for new staff, too. Consider having all new staff members attend your volunteer orientation and training sessions.

Creating a Comprehensive Volunteer Training Program

Most shelters find it helpful to provide a general animal-handling course for all volunteers. Chances are good that even volunteers who are only doing data-entry work will interact with animals in some way while at the shelter. Volunteers will need to have some basic knowledge of animal behavior and handling to assist and keep themselves, the public, and the animals safe.

In the general training session, volunteers should be told basic rules and expectations. Volunteers should know the "boundaries" of their work in the shelter and understand the consequences of not respecting those rules (see below). Be sure to talk as well about all of the benefits they receive as volunteers. Allow plenty of time for questions and discussion.

Keep these tips in mind when developing your volunteer training programs:

- **Tailor the training to the job and be specific.** Even tasks that seem easy, such as dog walking, require thorough training. Volunteers who are new to the shelter environment may not know how to read animal behavior or control the spread of disease. Volunteers with pets at home may come in thinking they "know cats and dogs" and don't need comprehensive training; however, they may never have interacted with large, stressed, unsocialized, and unpredictable animals who don't behave as do their own pets. No matter what the volunteer's stated experience, require all volunteers to attend general training and special training for their respective jobs.

■ **Teach volunteers all the basics.** Volunteers need to know how critical disease control is to every shelter. Be sure to teach them to wash their hands before handling each animal and how important it is to keep animals separated. Also teach basic tasks, including how to remove animals from their kennels safely to avoid injury (to the volunteer or animal).

■ **Write it down.** The more written, posted procedures you can offer volunteers, the better your program will be. Volunteers usually work one day a week at the most, so it will take longer for them to remember basic protocols. Step-by-step instructions help, even for some of the simplest tasks. Written protocols allow volunteers to take initiative (and not interrupt the staff every five minutes with a question about how a task should be completed). One great training tool is *How to Do Almost Anything in the Shelter* (Humane Society of the United States 2002).

■ **Set clear boundaries.** Explicitly teach and show volunteers which animals they can work with and which they cannot. Volunteers should not handle animals being held for rabies quarantine, unadoptable animals, animals with severe medical or behavior problems (such as aggression), or animals scheduled for euthanasia. Help volunteers understand why these limitations exist and how decisions are made about animals. The staff and management of the organization, not the volunteers, should decide the disposition of animals at the shelter. Volunteers should be expected to support such decisions and keep the decisions confidential.

■ **Be creative.** Adults learn in a variety of ways, so try to use different training techniques. These can include visual aids, role-play, and learning by doing. Animal Care Training Programs (*www.4act.com:* click on *Additional Resources*) offers a helpful series of training tapes for animal shelter staff and volunteers.

■ **Take charge.** It is crucial that volunteers understand the hierarchy of leadership: who is in charge and who has the final say. Don't walk on eggshells with your volunteers. While volunteer integration is important to make the program work, volunteers need to understand through training that their role is one of support, not goal setting, policy making, or program direction.

■ **Teach tools of the trade.** To be successful, volunteers need to have appropriate tools (for example, grooming supplies) and know how to use them. Find an accessible area where items can be stored for easy access by volunteers.

■ **Cross-train your volunteers.** Cross-training helps volunteers fill in other jobs as needed. It also broadens their understanding of the organization and can increase your organization's scheduling flexibility.

■ **Test their knowledge.** If volunteers know they will be tested, they may be more likely to pay attention, and an occasional "pop quiz" gives you the added benefit of peace of mind, once you know your volunteers understand what to do.

■ **Keep records of who has been trained in which areas.** You'll want to make sure each volunteer has completed his or her full training requirements before being let loose in the shelter. This information should be indicated in each volunteer's personnel file.

■ **Remember your full-timers.** Make sure your staff receives at least the same level of training as do your volunteers (see chapter 10).

■ **Designate a "trial period."** For a smooth volunteer transition into the organization, consider designating a trial period in which all new volunteers are considered to be "in training." This gives staff a chance to observe new volunteers and to feel free to provide guidance without worrying about offending them. Volunteers "in training" can wear a special badge to allow others to identify them and help them feel welcome. Consider having a review meeting with volunteers when they complete their "in training" period to see how the job is working out for them.

■ **Consider color-coding volunteers.** The Humane Society of Austin and Travis County (Texas) color-codes the dogs at the shelter based on behavior issues and codes its volunteers to match! To ensure consistency of handling, all new volunteers, regardless of their experience, start out being coded "green," with access only to the most tractable dogs. Volunteers must achieve milestones (such as a certain number of hours volunteered) and attend training classes to be permitted to handle more challenging dogs, who have been assigned to the next color-coded level, and so on.

■ **Use volunteer trainers.** Once the program is up and running, consider using well-trained volunteers to teach new volunteers the ropes. Continuing education is as important for volunteers as it is for staff. Keep in mind that the more you increase a volunteer's responsibilities, the more time staff members must spend training the volunteer. Experienced, well-trained volunteer mentors can make this training easier. At the Seattle Animal Shelter, the volunteer program is implemented by a large group of volunteer team leaders. The volunteer manager helps coordinate the team leaders, but the leaders are in charge of their own programs and recruit, train, and supervise the volunteers beneath them. This setup has proven to be very successful for the shelter and helps take some of the coordinating burden off the volunteer manager.

Developing the Volunteer Manual

One of the first training tools you will need to develop is your volunteer manual, which should include policies and procedures to help you manage the program and give volunteers a head start in learning about the organization. The manual provides a great training tool and serves as a good reference for volunteers. It should include information to help volunteers feel "in the know" and enable them to assist visitors; the content should also empower volunteers to function independently within the guidelines of the organization.

The volunteer manual should be friendly, welcoming, and warm while still conveying the importance of the organization's policies. You don't want to overburden volunteers with too many rules and policies but creating some structure is necessary. A good place to start is your employee manuals and your written standard operating procedures. (If you don't have such tools for staff, then reread chapter 1.) Sample volunteer manuals are available on the HSUS web site for shelters at *www.AnimalSheltering.org*; these may serve as models for your own manual.

When creating your manual, consider including the following:

- **A welcome letter** from the executive director or governing leadership of the organization. A simple welcome letter thanking volunteers for dedicating their time to your organization sets a friendly tone for the manual.

- **The organization's mission statement.** Volunteers who choose to spend their time helping your cause should have a clear understanding of the organization's mission and goals. If you develop a separate mission statement for the volunteer program, include that as well. It should be clear to all volunteers where your organization is heading and what it is striving to accomplish. After all, the volunteers are there to help you meet those goals!

- **A brief history of your organization and its achievements.** No doubt your shelter is proud of its many accomplishments. Tell volunteers about them! Not only will the history lesson give volunteers a sense of pride, but it also will help them see just what can be accomplished by dedicating the proper time and resources.

- **A list of services your shelter provides.** Do you offer pet-loss support groups? Do you have a low-cost spay/neuter program? Do you provide animal control services to the community? Volunteers may not be familiar with all your organization has to offer the community. Briefly describe each of your programs and services.

■ **Description of shelter policies.** Provide an overview of some of your main operating policies and procedures. Explaining the requirements of your adoption process and the length of your holding period will help volunteers understand the "hows" and "whys" of what you do and will help prevent misunderstandings. Make it clear that volunteers are expected to adhere to the organization's position and serve as its representatives.

■ **Organizational philosophy on sensitive issues.** Volunteers need to know the organization's philosophical stance on complex issues that face the animal-sheltering community. Euthanasia is a prime example. It's essential for volunteers to understand generally how euthanasia decisions are made and what method is used. Even if your shelter is limited admission (or, in more common but less accurate terms, "no-kill"), animals may still need to be euthanized if they become ill or aggressive. Some shelters have found it helpful to draw up one statement clearly outlining why euthanasia decisions shouldn't be questioned and another "compassion" statement explaining why it is hard for staff to be questioned about these decisions.

■ **Hours of operation.** Are the adoption hours different from the general operating hours? On which holidays is the shelter closed to the public? List all hours and days of operation so volunteers not only know when to show up but also can educate the public. If off-hours volunteering is permitted, specify the hours that volunteers can work at the shelter when it's closed to the public.

■ **A list of important phone numbers and other contact information.** Provide a list of all staff work extensions, particularly those for staff who supervise or work with volunteers. Be sure to include your organization's address and web site as well. Do you use e-mail? If so, provide appropriate e-mail addresses that volunteers can use to reach key personnel—particularly the director of volunteers.

■ **Organizational chart.** Including an organizational chart provides a great visual picture of how the shelter is structured and who reports to whom. Are your volunteers included on your organizational chart? They should be! Also clearly explain how the organization is structured and funded. Are you a nonprofit with a board of directors, or are you a department of the local government funded by tax dollars?

■ **A map of the building.** Help volunteers get the lay of the land. Include a copy of the building floor plan in the manual and indicate areas that are off-limits to volunteers, such as the rabies-quarantine areas and euthanasia room.

■ **Statistics.** Consider providing animal intake, adoption, and euthanasia statistics for the past year. It may be helpful to include statistics about the number of calls the shelter receives or the number of requests for assistance animal control responds to each month. Any statistics that provide a broader picture of the organization and how many services you offer are helpful to volunteers and will make them better advocates for your cause.

■ **Volunteer position descriptions.** Include a list of positions available to volunteers and the duties and skills required for each one.

■ **Volunteer rights, responsibilities, and privileges.** Clearly spell out what's expected of your volunteers as well as what they can expect—respect and appreciation—in return.

■ **Scheduling and sign-in procedures.** Make sure volunteers know how to schedule their volunteer time and that they're expected to show up for their shift. Provide instructions for signing in and out to ensure accurate tracking of donated time. Is there a minimum overall time commitment? Do you want volunteers to commit to a minimum of ten hours per month for six months? If so, indicate this clearly. Who should a volunteer notify if he or she is sick or otherwise cannot make it to an assigned shift?

■ **Training requirements and the "in training" period.** If all new volunteers must complete an "in training" period, explain that in your manual. Include a description of what training is offered and required. As a benefit of volunteering, will volunteers be permitted to attend training sessions provided to the staff? If so, state in the manual that such benefits are available.

■ **General animal handling and behavior information.** Consider providing a list of dos and don'ts when working with animals at the shelter. You can also include a glossary of common terms volunteers may hear in the shelter, such as the names of various diseases. Such written information should be provided in conjunction with a comprehensive training program.

■ **Reimbursements to volunteers.** If volunteers transport animals to off-site adoption centers or wildlife rehabilitators as part of their duties, they should be offered reimbursement for their mileage. Reimbursement qualifications should be detailed in the manual.

■ **Confidentiality policy.** If they work in the shelter, volunteers may have access to computer records and other information that may be confidential. Clearly state that volunteers are not permitted to share such information with others.

- **Evaluation procedures.** Will volunteers be reviewed annually? Is there an initial review after the specified "in training" period? Explain your evaluation procedures so volunteers know what to expect.

- **Policy on work attire.** Is there a dress code for volunteers? Do you expect your volunteers to wear a special smock, T-shirt, or name tag during their shifts that identifies them as volunteers? Explain reasons for dress codes: for example, long pants (not shorts) protect skin from animal scratches and nonskid, rubber-soled shoes protect against falls on slippery kennel floors.

- **Policy on personal belongings.** Tell volunteers that the shelter provides a place for volunteers to store their coats and other personal belongings. Recommend that volunteers keep valuables with them or locked in their vehicles. Include a notice that the organization is not responsible for personal items left in the shelter.

- **Policy on visitors and personal guests.** Your manual should explain that unless the friend is also a volunteer with your organization, volunteers cannot bring friends along on their shifts to "help out." Also explain that volunteers should not bring their children to the shelter. Clearly outline what's acceptable so you don't end up with any surprise guests tagging along with volunteers during their shifts.

- **Sexual harassment policy and antidiscrimination policy.** The policies in place for staff hold true for volunteers with regard to sexual harassment and discrimination. Be sure to include a copy of such policies for volunteers.

- **Parking policy.** Are there designated areas where volunteers should park? Are parking permits required in any areas?

- **Alcohol and drug policy.** Clearly state that any volunteer under the influence of alcohol or drugs will not be permitted on the property.

- **Description of designated eating and smoking areas.** How often are breaks allowed? Can volunteers take breaks in the staff break room? If not, be sure to tell them where they can go to unwind.

- **Safety information.** State which vaccinations are recommended or required for volunteers who have direct contact with animals in the shelter. Include general information on disease control and recognition. Also include fire alarm and evacuation procedures. (For more on safety issues, see chapter 9.)

- **What to do if bitten or scratched.** State clearly that any volunteer who has been bitten or scratched must report the incident immediately to a staff member. Since many volunteers are afraid to report scratches or bites to protect an animal from being euthanized for rabies testing, stress the seriousness of rabies and other animal-related health and safety concerns. Explain the quarantine process. Stress that for the safety of the volunteer and all others, failure to report such incidents will result in the volunteer's termination.

- **Grievance policy.** Outline the chain of command so volunteers can report concerns to the appropriate staff member. Detail the steps they can take to make complaints and let the volunteers know that you take their problems seriously.

- **Tax deductions.** Volunteers may be eligible to claim deductions on their tax returns for travel time to and from volunteer assignments. You may want to mention this in your manual and encourage volunteers to check with their tax advisor.

- **Media information.** Tell volunteers how to respond to media. For example, if a reporter approaches or contacts a volunteer, what should the volunteer do? Is he or she permitted to speak on behalf of the organization? Or should the volunteer refer the reporter to a designated spokesperson?

- **A "FAQ" (frequently asked questions) page.** Providing volunteers with a page or two of frequently asked questions and answers is a great reference. Including the answers to the most common questions will keep you from having to repeat them.

- **Termination policy.** Explain that volunteers should tell the volunteer coordinator or other designated staff if they intend to stop volunteering for any reason. Encourage departing volunteers to provide feedback, which can help you improve your program. State how much you value their work and remind volunteers to discuss any concerns or grievances with the volunteer manager. Providing volunteers with these instructions will help you make the volunteer's resignation smoother—and may even cause him or her to reconsider leaving!

Remember that you will need to monitor, review, and update policies frequently for both staff and volunteers. Things change, so flexibility and frequent updates are important to ensure the accuracy of your policies.

Chapter 7

Scheduling and Record Keeping

Why Do You Need a Schedule?

Part of managing volunteers is mastering the art of juggling schedules. Without a schedule, a host of problems can develop. Staff may not know when to expect volunteers (it's difficult to complete a project if no one shows up). Too many volunteers may decide to come in at once and end up overwhelming the staff, or volunteers with identical jobs may show up at the same time. They may even think you don't need them and stop coming altogether.

Creating a schedule helps you avoid these situations and see who is (and is not) coming in; a schedule also helps you evaluate where help is lacking.

How Strict Should the Schedule Be?

Some positions may not require scheduling at all. For example, some organizations permit volunteers who socialize cats to come and go as they please rather than adhering to a specific schedule. Other positions may need a schedule—adoption counseling or front desk volunteer—so you are sure to have enough help when you need it. Your schedule should be tailored to the needs of your organization as well as the volunteers' availability.

In a 2001 study of executive volunteers at the March of Dimes (Farmer and Fedor 2001), researchers found that when an organization's demands on a volunteer interfered with family life and paid work activities, volunteer commitment decreased: volunteers worked fewer hours per month and donated less money. "Being sensitive to scheduling difficulties, and (especially) to the way in which the demands placed upon volunteers can negatively spillover into their work and home roles, should be a priority for volunteer organizations' paid staff," suggests the researchers (Farmer and Fedor 2001, 14).

Volunteer time needs to be spent wisely and respectfully. Never waste it. You need to preplan assignments before volunteers arrive to ensure there will be meaningful work waiting for them during their shifts. And if there isn't any work for a volunteer to do, call him or her before the shift. Work with each volunteer to develop a schedule that works for that individual. That way, volunteers are more likely to arrive when they promise, and they can fit their duties into a schedule that doesn't interfere with other obligations. The more you can accommodate volunteers' busy lives, the more likely they are to give you what you need. Volunteers will appreciate your efforts, thereby helping to bolster dedication to your program.

How to Create a Schedule

When developing a schedule, work with staff first to determine when and how many volunteers are needed for each position. Then recruit for each time slot you need filled.

If you already have volunteers coming in at will, without a schedule, work with them to implement one. Explain that you want to maximize their time and that you need them to help you identify and plan which shifts they will work. Allow them to choose the times that work best for them and meet your needs as well. Volunteers are more likely to cooperate with new procedures if they feel they've had a say in how those procedures are developed.

At the Capital Area Humane Society, the volunteer coordinator doesn't create a schedule. Instead, she maintains a white board in her office where staff can list projects needing volunteer help. Volunteers know to check the board, pick a task, and seek the staff member who listed it. This method provides a great opportunity for staff to seek volunteer help and for volunteers to choose what jobs they want to do.

Sign-in Procedures and Time Sheets

All volunteers should sign in at the beginning of their shifts and sign out at the end on a sheet that's accessible to all of them. Not only will this help you to keep track of who is coming in as scheduled and who is missing assignments but it also will be invaluable for personnel safety. (You want to know who is in the building in case of a fire or other emergency.)

Consider placing a volunteer sign-in bulletin board in a well-traveled area, preferably away from public view. Such a volunteer sign-in area can also serve as an information and communication center for posted notices about pertinent policy changes or events and volunteer recognition. However, it only works if the information on the board is kept current! If you stop updating it, volunteers may stop checking it and forget to sign in.

In addition to a sign-in sheet, consider having each volunteer submit a time sheet regularly to help you track individual contributions to the organization. Time sheets are particularly important for off-site volunteers, including those who maintain your web site from home or who conduct humane education programs at local schools. Since these volunteers cannot sign in and out on your master log at the shelter, you need a way to include their hours in your records.

It can be difficult to track hours for some positions, such as foster care. You may need to develop some simple formulas for crediting such volunteer positions. For example, the Capital Area Humane Society credits fosterers with two hours of volunteer work per day while fostering an animal to compensate for care, feeding, and socialization.

Capital Area Humane Society
DAILY VOLUNTEER LOG SHEET

DATE:

	VOLUNTEER NAME (PRINT CLEARLY)	WHAT YOU DID TODAY	TIME IN	TIME OUT	TOTAL
1					
2					
3					
4					
5					
6					
7					
8					
9					
10					
11					
12					
13					
14					
15					
16					
17					
18					
19					
20					
21					
22					
23					
24					
25					
26					

MONADNOCK HUMANE SOCIETY
VOLUNTEER DEPARTMENT
VOLUNTEER LOG

NAME OF VOLUNTEER: _____

(LAST)   (FIRST)

PHONE: _____

(AREA CODE) – (NUMBER)

EMERGENCY CONTACT: _____ **PHONE**: _____

DATE	TIME IN	TIME OUT	JOB CODE
1/18/03	10:00 am	12:00 pm	GO

DATE	TIME IN	TIME OUT	JOB CODE

Tracking Individual Volunteer Records

It's important to keep a file for every volunteer; consider including the following in each file:

- The volunteer's basic contact information, including emergency contact and physician

- Any relevant personal information, including birthday, spouse's name, and pets' names

- A copy of the completed volunteer application

- A signed permission form to conduct reference or background checks (if your organization uses such checks)

- A copy of the job description

- Signed volunteer agreement

- Signed liability waiver (see chapter 9)

- The assigned schedule and any information detailing general availability

- Summary of hours worked and time sheets

- A list of completed training

- Any performance reviews, documents detailing problems, discussions, and achievement recognition. (Like staff performance, volunteer performance should be evaluated.)

Such files should be kept for all active volunteers. Ellis and Noyes (1990) suggest keeping such files for five years after the volunteer has left the organization. That should be sufficient documentation in case of an IRS audit or insurance question. It's a good idea to keep inactive volunteers on your general organizational mailing list so they continue to receive your newsletter and fund-raising mailings! (Of course, share your list of active volunteers with your fund-raising staff, too.)

Overall Program Data to Track

To determine what kind of data to track, decide first what you want to know about your program. Do you want to know the number of on-site or off-site hours volunteers have contributed? Do you want to track volunteer retention and turnover rates for the year? Do you want to know how much money volunteers have raised? Do you want to know how many adoptions volunteers facilitated and the number of follow-up calls they made after adoption? Once you've determined what you want to know, it's easier to develop a tracking system.

So often, when asked how successful an organization's volunteer program is, the director responds proudly by saying something like, "We have fifty volunteers who contributed over five hundred hours last year." Does the director know what was actually accomplished during those hours? Rather than simply adding up the hours volunteers contributed, try to quantify their efforts. What you really want to know is *how* your volunteers helped your cause.

Tracking such data doesn't require an advanced degree, just a little advance planning and organization. In fact, the simpler your tracking system, the more consistent volunteers will be in tracking their activities. The benefits of having program data are enormous. Recording the accomplishments of your volunteers can help you obtain funding from foundations, individual donors, and the local government. A review of accomplishments also motivates volunteers and encourages involvement of staff, who can see direct evidence of volunteer participation. Consider using the data as part of your annual report to highlight your volunteer program.

Need some ideas to get you started? Consider measuring:

- **Number of volunteers involved during the past year** (with a good tracking program, these data can be broken down by gender, ethnicity, age, etc., as needed).

- **Number of total volunteer hours contributed.** (It may also be helpful to determine the total monetary value of your volunteers' time. According to the Independent Sector [*IndependentSector.org*], the dollar value of volunteer time was $17.19 per hour for 2003.)

- **Number of animals and people volunteers helped and in what ways.** (For example, if you have a foster care program, how many animals did volunteers foster who were later adopted into new homes?)

- **Monetary donations from volunteers.** Consider in-kind donations of equipment and supplies from volunteers as well as out-of-pocket expenses for which volunteers decline reimbursement.

- **Volunteer activities and successes.** Stories of volunteers helping animals can be used for fund-raising and recognition events.

Volunteer Management Software

A wide range of software programs can help you track this information and other data for your volunteer program. Many shelters who use Volunteer Works by Red Ridge report great success. The cost of the software is close to $1,000, but the time and effort it saves may be well worth the price tag. For details about the program's features, check out *www.redridge.com* (click on "Volunteer Works").

The Raiser's Edge fund-raising software by Black Baud also has a volunteer component that some shelters have found helpful. For more information on the software, visit *www.blackbaud.com/solutions/raisersedge.asp*. Samaritan Technologies (*www.samaritan.com*) offers customizable volunteer management software free for nonprofits with fewer than one hundred volunteers. Volunteer Software (*www.volsoft.com*) offers its Volunteer Reporter software for approximately $700. The E-Volunteerism web site contains an article on the various volunteer management software programs available; visit *http://e-volunteerism.com/quarterly/02win/web2b.php*. (To obtain the complete article, you must either be a member of the e-volunteerism journal or purchase a copy online for $3.)

Chapter 8

Working with Young Volunteers

This chapter is based on materials and publications developed by The National Association of Humane and Environmental Education (NAHEE), the youth education division of The Humane Society of the United States. For more information on service learning and humane education programs, visit NAHEE online at www.nahee.org.

Do You Want to Involve Kids in Your Volunteer Program?

Incorporating kids into a volunteer program can prove to be challenging. On the one hand, a youth volunteer program provides a unique opportunity to help young citizens grow into better educated, compassionate adults; responsible pet caregivers; and supporters of animal protection. On the other hand, inviting kids to work in the shelter requires a much greater level of supervision and more tightly structured activities and involves more liability.

It may be tempting for shelters to simply require that all volunteers be at least eighteen years old to participate, but compelling evidence demonstrates why you should seriously consider involving younger people in your volunteer programs. Consider the following statistics from Independent Sector (2001):

- Forty-four percent of adults volunteer, and two-thirds of these volunteers began volunteering their time when they were young.

- Adults who began volunteering as young people are twice as likely to volunteer as those who did not volunteer when they were younger.

- In every income and age group, those who volunteered as young people give and volunteer more than those who did not.

- Those who volunteered as young people, and whose parents volunteered, became the most generous adults in giving time.

These statistics certainly provide a strong argument for youth involvement. And youth are already involved in volunteer service to a large extent. In fact, a recent Independent Sector study (2001) revealed that more than half of all teens (59.3 percent) volunteer somewhere; their charitable activities cover everything from health and human services to education and protecting the environment. In 1995 13.3 million teenagers gave 2.4 billion hours of volunteer time: sorting and handing out food for the homeless; painting over graffiti; tutoring and coaching; restoring wildlife habitats; and organizing pet-food drives. Forty-one percent of teens each contributed an average of $82 of their own money to charitable organizations.

These findings have important implications for grassroots organizations, because they can benefit in so many ways from young people's enthusiasm for delivering needed services to the community. This is particularly important for animal care and control agencies because so much interest and ethical concern among teenagers focuses on animal protection.

What Are the Roadblocks to Involving Youth?

The potential pitfalls of managing a youth program—scheduling problems, dropout rates, and staff-volunteer conflicts—mirror those encountered in any volunteer program. Running a successful program requires significant investment of time and resources in planning, organizing, training, supervising, and evaluating. Working with teens raises additional issues as well. Do local laws limit the number of hours a minor may volunteer? Does your insurance cover minors? Do special provisions cover teens working off-site, such as at your annual dog walk? What about riding in your shelter's vehicle?

Opinions vary widely regarding whether to welcome teen volunteers and what kinds of tasks they should be given. Animal care and control organizations sometimes avoid young volunteers because of the associated risks and liability issues or because they feel teens can be unreliable, difficult to supervise, difficult to schedule, or unable (or unwilling) to make a long-term commitment.

Some agencies require a parent or guardian to accompany youngsters during their volunteer shift, an arrangement requiring extra supervision for that extra individual. Other agencies restrict youth involvement to a well-structured humane education program or "camp" where the goal is education rather than hands-on assistance.

Research your options. Weigh the costs and benefits to determine if starting a youth program is a good move for your organization. If the answer is no, don't let that stop you from collaborating with young people. There are many worthwhile ways of involving teens in your work with minimal risk and only a small investment of time. For example, instead of developing a formal, full-blown youth program and involving young people in direct care of animals, concentrate on enlisting teens' help with individual projects, such as an advocacy campaign, fund-raising drive, or public awareness initiative. Check with local schools about "service-learning" programs, an excellent way of reaping the benefits of working with young people while at the same time avoiding some of the pitfalls—risk and liability issues, drop-out rates, and problems associated with reliability, punctuality, and supervision.

What Is Service Learning?

Service learning is an educational model—a way of learning that lets students engage in meaningful community service as long as it relates to what they are learning in a particular class. Ideally, what kids are learning in the classroom should help them complete the service component of the program, and the service component should add to students' knowledge of the academic subject. So, in the process of serving their communities, students gain practical knowledge of the subjects they're studying: foreign culture, history, environmental protection, computer science, social studies—whatever the subject may be. By connecting students to their communities, service learning produces better, more active learners and more involved citizens.

Due largely to federal initiatives aimed at increasing youth service (including the National and Community Service Act of 1990, which provides schools with grants), schools in all fifty states now have service-learning programs. According to the National Center for Education Statistics (U.S. Department of Education 1999), during the 1998–99 academic year, 83 percent of U.S. high schools had students participating in some form of community service; 71 percent arranged community-service opportunities for students; and 46 percent had students participating in service-learning programs.

Many of the projects students might undertake for your organization lend themselves to the service-learning concept because the tasks are so easy to integrate with academic work. Students in computer and media labs and art and photography clubs, for example, often have access to state-of-the-art equipment and know how to use it. These students can help develop or update your web site and newsletter; help with graphic design; create school bulletin boards with photos and descriptions of animals up for adoption; and script and produce public service announcements to air on public-access television. With help from its school's video production class, a club of twenty high school students from Tacoma, Washington, produced a four-minute educational video, *Protect Your Pet! Spay or Neuter,* that was distributed to schools and television stations. The club's mentor and education director at Mt. Tacoma Humane Society (where much of the footage was shot) uses the video in his humane-education presentations.

Young people can represent your shelter effectively at adoption sites and special events; organize collections of pet food and supplies in their communities; set up information tables in school cafeterias; and staff booths at conferences and exhibits.

There are five key benefits of a service-learning program:

1. **It helps you fill a real need in the community**, by increasing pet adoptions, for example, or promoting responsible pet care.

2. **It provides a variety of assignments.** Students are expected to gain practical knowledge of the subjects they are studying, such as computer science, social studies, physical education, or language arts. Your shelter can recruit teens for many different tasks, not simply for animal care.

3. **It attracts kids inclined to practice good citizenship.** Young people who demonstrate initiative, concern, responsibility, teamwork, and involvement in public life are an asset to you and your community.

4. **It is generally long term.** Students must commit a certain number of hours to your organization, often over the course of a semester or a school year. That helps minimize problems such as poor attendance, tardiness, and dropping out. Because teachers, not your staff, are primarily responsible for ensuring that students meet their obligations, you do not have to act as an "enforcer."

5. **It helps you gain energetic advocates for your cause.** Students think, write, and talk about their experiences, using journals, articles, reports, photos, videos, group discussions, speeches, and presentations. As they reflect on what they have learned from and contributed to your organization, they also share their knowledge and experience with schoolmates, family, and others in the community.

It's easy to see how working with a service-learning program can help you avoid some of the problems normally associated with youth volunteers in the shelter. Just remember to make sure the tasks students perform for your shelter meet not just your needs but the students' needs, too.

How to Start a Service-Learning Program

Determining your shelter's needs and identifying duties suitable for young people will help you develop a clear strategy. As with your main volunteer program, clear job descriptions and defined roles are crucial to successful relationships with these students.

Next, consider your training and support needs. Perhaps you should visit other shelters that take advantage of service-learning programs. Learn as much as you can about what other shelters do, what works and what doesn't. In your planning process, involve people from your community, including teachers, school administrators, and teens themselves.

The Independent Sector's study on youth volunteerism (2001) revealed that teen volunteers initially get involved through school (50 percent) and/or a religious institution (53 percent). Browse through schools' web sites to glean preliminary information about their clubs, youth service activities, and courses with a service-learning component; these pages often include the names of faculty advisors you can contact. Many schools maintain a list of possible community service sites; ask to have your shelter represented in such lists.

Another way of finding out about your local service-learning programs is to get in touch with the State Education Agency (SEA), which distributes funds to local school districts in most of the fifty states, Washington, D.C., and Puerto Rico. You can find them online at *www.learnandserve.org/about/sea.html*.

Once you've recruited a few students to fulfill their service-learning requirements with your organization, they can help you find more students. Teens are four times more likely to volunteer if they are asked than if they are not: 93 percent of teens who are asked to volunteer end up doing so; of those who are not asked, only 24 percent volunteer. You are the "headhunter" in this scenario, appealing to students with the message, "We need your ideas. Would you and a couple of your friends be willing to help us get started?"

Tips for Successfully Working With Young Volunteers

Screen kids and teens just as you would adults. Require a commitment and give them clear job descriptions. Young people like working as a team and need opportunities to develop friendships. For this reason, you might ask your young volunteers to stuff envelopes or collate adoption send-home kits in a conference room with a pizza and a movie. This kind of work does not involve direct contact with animals, so you may have the added benefit of fewer liability concerns. Try to make service time fun, but don't lose control and let it become the social hour. Important work still needs to be accomplished.

Keep in mind, too, that the work must be meaningful. Involve young people in decision making; give them plenty of interesting, challenging, and satisfying assignments; and make clear how their work fulfills your shelter's mission. According to Independent Sector (2001), teens have a higher volunteer rate if they believe they have a moral duty to help—and if they believe they can help to overcome social problems through their volunteer efforts.

Teaming up with young people, especially those who are dedicated to helping animals, can revive your passion for animal protection and bring new spirit to your cause. Whether you've established a youth program, are in the early planning stages of such a program, or are simply seeking young people's input and involvement from time to time, trade ideas and information with other animal care and control organizations. Share materials and discuss common setbacks and practical solutions. Working with young people presents unique possibilities, and networking with other animal protection groups can go a long way toward making the most of those opportunities.

Here are some additional tips to help you succeed with young volunteers:

■ **Make a match.** Does the project fit a young person's particular skills? A simple way to determine students' interests is to engage youth volunteers in an informal interview or quick questionnaire. Some animal care and control agencies post volunteer interest forms online. You can also do a quick scan of other shelters' web sites for ideas on how to write your own questionnaire.

■ **Make it meaningful.** Young people, like all volunteers, need to feel a sense of accomplishment and know they are respected. Seek input from young volunteers and get them involved in problem solving and project development. It is important to allow them some autonomy and decision-making power.

■ **Provide feedback.** Evaluate students' performance, give constructive feedback, and provide ongoing training and supervision.

■ **Keep them informed.** Student volunteers should know what's going on in your organization, so keep them updated through newsletters, memos, e-mails, and office discussions. Explain budget issues so teens don't assume your budget is limitless!

■ **Keep in touch.** Keeping in touch with parents and teachers (through phone calls, e-mails, fliers, permission slips, handwritten notes, and so on) helps them understand how their children are contributing to your organization, thereby making them more supportive.

■ **Keep records.** Maintaining accurate records can be especially important in service-learning programs, where proof of hours and assignments is often required.

For More Information

■ **Youth Activism Project** (*www.youthactivism.com*). Mega-Planner Toolkit is a comprehensive resource that includes *Maximum Youth Involvement: The Complete Gameplan for Community Action*, a 170-page manual that answers nearly one hundred questions on how adults and organizations can support young people as effective advocates. The Toolkit also includes a 130-page handbook, *Youth! The 26% Solution*, that offers step-by-step strategies for students and adult allies on everything from organizing a small meeting to wording a petition, capturing media coverage, and interacting with public officials. The Toolkit costs $35.00.

- **Pitch In** (*www.pitchin.org*) is an e-zine dedicated to discussing volunteerism by youth.

- **Open up opportunities for service learning at your shelter** by signing up at SERVEnet (*www.servenet.org*), a program of Youth Service America. Fill out the organizational profile to become a member of the network, which enables you to post notices and recruit volunteers. Youth Corps for Animals (*www.youthforanimals.org*) also hosts a site where animal protection groups can advertise their volunteering needs. Both services are free.

- **Do you know of a teen activist who deserves special recognition?** Have you piloted a youth program you're proud of? Share your good news with HumaneTeen (*www.humaneteen.org*). The first animal-protection site designed exclusively for teenagers, HumaneTeen features true stories of young activists and student clubs from around the country. The site welcomes information from animal care and control agencies about youth who have made a difference for animals in their communities. HumaneTeen includes interactive features, such as a survey that lets teens sound off on animal-protection issues and see how others voted. (Survey topics change regularly.) "Speak Up!" gives young people a chance to express their opinions and publish original poetry on animal and environmental topics. HumaneTeen also offers downloadable resources, such as "Student Action Guide," a step-by-step manual for teens who want to form animal-protection clubs, and resource books for high-school students on topics ranging from factory farming to animal cruelty and research. These publications are available in print form as well and may be ordered through the HSUS Youth Education Division, 67 Norwich Essex Turnpike, East Haddam, CT 06423, 860-434-8666.

Chapter 9

Keeping Volunteers Safe

Your organization needs to take responsibility for keeping staff and volunteers safe at all times. That's where risk management comes into play. "Risk management" may seem like a daunting term, but it's really just common sense and involves keeping staff and volunteers out of harm's way through sound policies, procedures, and training.

Chances are good that you're already practicing it to some degree—or, if you're following the advice put forth in this manual, you've at least made a good start. Good risk-management strategies include many of the things discussed in previous chapters: developing clear job descriptions that carefully outline volunteers' duties; recruiting volunteers who are capable of performing the needed tasks; and volunteer training that includes a review of the rules and safety protocols of the organization.

"Contrary to common belief, risk management isn't just about buying insurance. It isn't just about avoiding lawsuits," write Herman and Jackson (2001),

> It *is* about protecting and conserving your organization's resources and providing goods and services sensibly. Risk management frees your organization to pursue its mission by allowing your organization to take more—not less—risk. The difference is that your approach to risk can be structured and calculated rather than haphazard. (3)

The more you manage the potential risks, the safer your organization is likely to be. Practicing good risk management is important for another reason as well: it can improve the public's perceptions of your organization. If you're looking out for your volunteers, you'll be seen as a good organization to donate time to; volunteers will feel valued enough to keep coming back.

How to Prevent Trouble

In case you haven't sat down to think about it for a while, here are a few of the many environmental risks animal shelter staff and volunteers face:

- Scared, aggressive, feral, or fractious animals
- Rabies-suspect animals
- Physical exertion (heavy lifting of dog food and animals)
- Animal bites and scratches
- Zoonotic diseases
- Slippery floors
- Medical supplies, including needles and vaccines

- Exposure to chemical cleaning supplies
- Potential access to controlled substances
- Loud noise (due to barking dogs)
- Blood-borne pathogens

How can you reduce the chance that volunteers and staff will get hurt?

- **Look for risks.** What could happen to volunteers performing the jobs you've developed for them, and what can you do to help prevent unwanted surprises from occurring? Also, what if something goes wrong? Do staff and volunteers know how to handle the situation? If a volunteer is badly bitten during his or her shift, are the volunteer and his or her co-workers trained in how to secure the animal and provide first aid?

  Many risks can be reduced by simply being aware of them. During cleaning, are the floors slippery? If so, purchase squeegees to keep the floors dry and safe—and inexpensive "Caution: Wet Floor" cones to serve as friendly warnings that extra caution is in order.

- **Develop good policies and procedures.** State your safety procedures clearly and make sure volunteers understand the risks associated with their jobs. Alleviate as many risks as possible through policies and guidelines. Make sure volunteers know what they can and cannot do; for example, they should know they cannot visit animals in quarantine for rabies observation.

- **Avoid putting volunteers in positions they can't handle.** Make sure a volunteer is appropriate for the position you are giving him or her. For example, if you have an elderly volunteer with a bad back trying to walk large, hyperactive dogs, you may be setting up the volunteer for injury. Determine the physical demands for each position and place people accordingly.

- **Maintain your "Material Safety Data Sheets" as required by law.** In compliance with Occupational Safety and Health Administration (OSHA) regulations, manufacturers or distributors of hazardous chemicals must create Material Safety Data Sheets (MSDSs). These sheets are designed to ensure that chemicals are evaluated and that employees and volunteers are aware of the potential dangers and methods of protection. MSDSs detail proper procedures for working with chemicals and substances by describing physical properties, toxicology, health effects, first aid, storage requirements, necessary protective equipment, and spill/leak protocols.

■ **Provide a first aid station and safety equipment.** Be prepared to treat accidents or injuries. Here's a checklist of some equipment that should be available to staff and volunteers working at an animal shelter:

- Basic first aid kit that includes bandages, ointments, and medicines for treating routine injuries
- Eyewash stations
- Fire extinguishers
- Gloves (various types, including rubber, latex, and animal-handling)
- Proper animal-handling equipment such as control poles, muzzles, cat shields, and nets (be sure all staff and volunteers are trained in how to use them)
- Evacuation plans in case of fire or other emergencies
- Eye protection for mixing chemicals such as cleaning solutions
- Ear protection (OSHA regulations state that when employees are exposed to 85 decibels or higher over an eight-hour period, ear protection must be available—and many dog kennels easily exceed this limit)
- Face masks

■ **Train your staff and volunteers well.** Are staff and volunteers bitten frequently by cats? Perhaps they're not handling the animals properly and it's time for more training. Take steps to minimize risk to your whole staff, paid or volunteer. Training on how to read animal behavior and how to handle animals at the shelter should be required for all staff and volunteers.

■ **Clearly identify staff and volunteers.** All volunteers should be clearly identified as volunteers. Make sure they dress appropriately and consider providing special aprons or T-shirts that identify them as volunteers. Identification badges are a must.

■ **Provide vaccination recommendations to volunteers and staff.** It's a good idea to ensure that all staff and volunteers are up-to-date on basic vaccinations such as tetanus. Some agencies offer rabies pre-exposure vaccinations to staff—and sometimes even to volunteers. Unfortunately, such preventives are often prohibitively expensive and not covered by insurance. If you work in the animal care and control field, however, the benefits of receiving the pre-exposure series far outweigh the costs. If you've potentially had contact with rabies, the therapy will be minimal if you've already been vaccinated. (If you would like to arrange pre-exposure vaccinations for your staff and volunteers, contact your physician or local health department to learn what the procedures are in your area.)

- **Protect staff and volunteers' own pets.** Encourage staff and volunteers to get their own pets examined and vaccinated to protect them from any illness or disease that may inadvertently be carried home from the shelter.

- **Consider risks to volunteers working off-site.** For example, if volunteers are taking dogs for walks on nearby trails, make sure the trails are well maintained to avoid trips and falls.

- **Involve everyone in managing risk.** Since staff and volunteers are performing the tasks, they often know best what risks they take and what can be done to reduce them. All staff and volunteers should watch for potential problems and be required to report any concerns to the appropriate supervisor.

Liability Waivers

Create a document that explains the risks that volunteers are likely to face in your shelter, especially when working with animals. If you bring volunteers under age eighteen on board, you need the signature of the parent or legal guardian. A signed liability waiver won't protect you completely, but it's good risk management. Such a waiver demonstrates that your organization is making a good-faith effort to reduce potential problems by ensuring that volunteers have been educated about the risks involved with their work.

Warn volunteers, but don't scare them. Tell volunteers about the policies you have in place to protect them; make it clear that volunteers must follow those policies for their own safety as well as the safety of the public, other volunteers, staff, and, of course, animals.

If you decide to use a liability waiver as a risk-management tool, consider including the following:

- The volunteer's name and contact information
- The name of the person the volunteer reports to
- A statement that the volunteer has received, read, and agreed to comply with your organization's purposes, policies, and rules, including your organization's volunteer manual
- A dated signature of the executive director or volunteer coordinator
- A dated signature of the volunteer

Be sure to have any signed documents reviewed by your organization's attorney before integrating them into your program.

Liability Insurance

Insurance coverage and legal obligations vary from shelter to shelter, so contact your agent and your local labor department to make sure your volunteer program is adequately protected. Generally, the Nonprofit Risk Management Center (Herman and Jackson 2001) recommends that your organization be covered for the following scenarios:

- A volunteer is injured on the job, and your organization needs to cover the cost of medical treatment. If the volunteer has health insurance, that should serve as his or her primary coverage, but make sure your insurance will cover your volunteers if necessary.

- A volunteer sues your organization because of injuries, claiming that your organization was negligent.

- A volunteer does something that causes your organization to be sued by a third party.

- A volunteer is involved in an auto accident while performing a volunteer job. In most cases, a volunteer's personal auto insurance covers accidents that occur while the individual is driving his or her own car to perform tasks for the organization. However, when a volunteer is driving an organization's vehicle, the organization's policy may provide coverage. As always, it's best to contact your insurance agent. Before permitting any volunteer to drive your organization's vehicle, make sure that your policy permits it and that the volunteer has a valid driver's license, auto insurance, and a good driving record.

Insurance can be expensive, but it is well worth the investment. If you find the extra insurance for volunteers to be more than you can afford, consider what it would cost if a volunteer were to sue you and you didn't have it.

Volunteers and staff alike need to have faith that the organization is looking out for them. Safety of the people working for you should be the number-one priority. Without them, how can you help the animals in your community? Without such risk management, you can damage your organization's reputation and even set yourself up for possible lawsuits.

For More Information on Staff and Volunteer Safety

- MSDS Online: *www.msdsonline.com*
- Cornell University: *http://msds.pdc.cornell.edu/msdssrch.asp*
- Vermont Safety Information Resources, Inc.: *http://hazard.com*
- National Institute for Occupational Safety and Health: *www.cdc.gov/niosh*
- Occupational Safety & Health Administration: *www.osha.gov*
- Nonprofit Risk Management Center: *www.nonprofitrisk.org*

Monadnock Humane Society
Volunteer Service Orientation Form

VOLUNTEER WAIVER

(Please Print)

_____

Last Name   *First Name*

    I, _____ (Please print your name), hereby acknowledge that I have voluntarily agreed to participate in the Volunteer/Community Service Program at Monadnock Humane Society. I am aware that this program will involve exposure to animals kept at the Monadnock Humane Society kennels and cat wards, and hereby release the Monadnock Humane Society from and against any and all liability arising out of or connected in any way with my participation in the program.

_____   _____

MHS Volunteer Signature   *Date*

_____   _____

Parent/Guardian Signature if under 18 years old   *Date*

THE HUMANE SOCIETY OF THE UNITED STATES®

Dallas Spay-Neuter and Animal Wellness Center

I acknowledge that I have read and fully understand the terms and conditions of the foregoing Volunteer Agreement and agree to comply with the same.

_____ I agree to release, discharge, indemnify and hold The HSUS harmless for any and all damage to my personal property while performing my volunteer services to The HSUS in a voluntary capacity.

_____ I recognize that in handling animals at The HSUS clinic there exists a risk of injury including personal, physical harm. On behalf of myself, my heirs, personal representatives and executors, I hereby release, discharge, indemnify and hold harmless The HSUS, its agents, servants and employees from any and all claims, causes of actions or demands, of any nature or cause connected with my Volunteer Agreement. This might include costs, attorney's fees and court costs incurred by The HSUS in connection with my volunteer services based on damages or injuries which may be incurred or sustained by me in any way. Such damages or injuries might include, but are not limited to, animal bites, accidents, injuries and personal property damage.

_____ I understand that public relations is an important part of volunteering at The HSUS. I, therefore, agree on behalf of myself, my heirs, personal representatives, and executors to allow The HSUS to use any photographs taken of me for use in public relations efforts. The HSUS will use reasonable efforts to notify me, but such notification is not a condition of the photograph's release for public relations purposes.

I acknowledge that I have read and fully understand the terms and conditions of the foregoing Volunteer Agreement and agree to comply with the same.

_____

Date   Signature of Volunteer   Signature of HSUS Representative

_____

Potter League for Animals

Volunteer Release Form

I, _____, hereby agree to accept a position as a volunteer worker for The Robert Potter League for Animals, Inc. (hereinafter referred to as "The Potter League"), and in so doing, I agree to comply with all of the policies, rules, and regulations which may be established from time to time by The Potter League. I understand that failure to do so many result in my immediate termination as a volunteer.

I acknowledge that my services are provided strictly on a volunteer basis, without any pay or compensation of any kind, and without any liability of any nature on behalf of The Potter League, all services to be performed by me at my own risk.

I recognize that in handling animals and performing other volunteer tasks, there exists a risk of injury including physical harm caused by the animals. On behalf of myself, my heirs, personal representatives, and executors, I hereby release, discharge, indemnify, and hold harmless The Potter League, its agents, servants, and employees from any and all claims, causes of action, or demands, of any nature or cause, including costs and attorney's fees incurred by The Potter League in connection with the same, based on damages or injuries which may be incurred, or sustained by me in any way connected with my services for The Potter League, including, but not limited to, animal bites, accidents, or injuries.

_____
Date   Signature of Volunteer (Parent/Guardian, if for minor child)

_____
                          Witness

I, _____, understand that public relations is an important part of volunteering at The Potter League. On behalf of myself, my heirs, personal representatives, and executors, allow The Potter League to use any photographs, films, videotapes, or other visual representations taken of me in volunteer service for use in public relations efforts.

_____
Date   Signature of Volunteer (Parent/Guardian, if for minor child)

_____
                          Witness

Chapter 10

Supervising Volunteers

Volunteers, just like staff, need and deserve ongoing guidance and supervision. Always try to remember that supervision really is—and should be—support.

The Role of the Volunteer Coordinator

A volunteer coordinator should serve as the human resources department of a volunteer program. Larger shelters may have paid coordinators, but smaller shelters usually give the job to a paid staff person who often wears other hats, such as a humane education coordinator or shelter manager. Still other organizations rely on a volunteer to serve as coordinator; however, these organizations must be committed to continuing the program should the volunteer leave the organization. Lack of continuity in overseeing volunteers can lead to major disruptions in the program.

Ideally, a full-time, salaried staff person should oversee the volunteer program because the time required to perform the job correctly is more than most volunteers can commit to. Most volunteers need to earn a living and cannot donate their talents on a full-time basis. Paying a salary allows the organization to set a predetermined number of hours per week during which the coordinator will be available, providing for more stability. A paid coordinator may have more credibility with the staff, so he or she may be more effective in expanding volunteer involvement.

The volunteer coordinator should work with the staff to create volunteer job descriptions, set goals, implement training programs, and provide ongoing program evaluation. The day-to-day management and training of individual volunteers falls primarily on the shoulders of the managers and staff members working side-by-side with volunteers. While the volunteer coordinator can lay the foundation for a successful program, he or she cannot be expected to individually manage, train, and evaluate every volunteer in the program. That's why frontline managers and staff must be committed to managing and working with volunteers.

"The major role of the modern Volunteer Program Manager is thus not working directly with volunteers save those she or he recruits to help in these processes," explain McCurley and Lynch (1996, 8–9). "Rather, effective Volunteer Program Managers focus their attentions on paid staff, securing top management support for volunteer efforts and helping individual staff do a good job of managing and retaining their volunteer helpers."

The volunteer coordinator also provides an important bridge between staff and volunteers within the organization, contributing structure, training, and recruitment skills. A volunteer coordinator serves as a mediator and problem solver when staff members have problems with volunteers or volunteers have concerns about staff. It's important to have a coordinator available to keep the program running smoothly and minimize misunderstandings. Ideally, the volunteer coordinator's office should be accessible to both staff and volunteers and his or her work schedule (and availability) known to all.

The volunteer coordinator should keep detailed records of the volunteer program to ensure continuity should he or she be unavailable or leave the position (see chapter 7 for more information on ensuring your program's stability).

A well-organized individual with experience managing a number of people and personalities should be chosen for the position. While this person will be responsible for running the program, he or she cannot be expected to ensure that volunteers are accepted by staff. As discussed in chapter 2, it is top-level management's role to set the tone for volunteer involvement and the policies to implement the program. The following pages contain sample job descriptions for full-time animal shelter volunteer coordinators.

Table 5

Staff Time Devoted to Managing Volunteers

Charities with a paid staff volunteer manager who devotes 100 percent of his or her time to volunteer management	1 in 8 (or 12.5 percent)
Charities with a paid staff person whose responsibility includes management of volunteers	62 percent
The median amount of time the paid staff volunteer coordinator in charities spends on volunteer management	30 percent

Full-time paid volunteer coordinators are few and far between. Most organizations rely on a volunteer or paid staff person with other responsibilities to squeeze in volunteer management as part of his or her responsibilities. This poses challenges for organizations wanting to maximize volunteer involvement.

Source: The Urban Institute 2004.

CAPITAL AREA HUMANE SOCIETY

JOB DESCRIPTION

TITLE: VICE PRESIDENT OF VOLUNTEERS AND CUSTOMER SERVICE

RESPONSIBLE TO: PRESIDENT

GENERAL SUMMARY: Responsible for all facets of the volunteer programs, customer service, all employee training and computer support.

TYPICAL DUTIES AND RESPONSIBILITIES:

■ CUSTOMER SERVICE
- Supervise and support the Adoption Counselor Coordinator and Adoption Counseling staff.
- Manage customer service interactions at all levels.
- Coordinate rewards/discipline with department supervisors.
- Reinforce and model S.A.V.E.S. initiative.
- Provide emotional and conflict resolution support for supervisors, managers and frontline employees as needed.

■ TRAINING
- Creation, purchase, coordination and implementation of all CAHS customer service, volunteer, computer and employee training.
- Maintain a uniform training system for all employees and volunteers.
- Training the trainers for all levels of shelter operations.

■ VOLUNTEERS
- Execute volunteer orientations on a monthly basis.
- Responsible for maintaining records of volunteer hours donated.
- Golden Paw Awards Dinner once a year for volunteer recognition: Coordinate with Special Events coordinator.
- Provide certificates and awards, other duties as required.
- Mentoring, supervising and supporting coordinators and volunteers.

■ COMPUTER SYSTEMS
- Supervise and support the Information Technology Coordinator.
- Provide guidance and direction for purchases, repairs and system changes.

■ GENERAL
- Provide budget forecast for IT, Adoption Counseling and Volunteer departments.
- Support strategic plan and departmental initiatives as needed.

General description of duties:
- *Maintain volunteer files.*
- *Provide volunteers as needed for shelter support.*
- *Manage employee and volunteer recognition and appreciation.*
- *Supervise and problem solve volunteer issues.*
- *Supervise and problem solve customer service issues at all levels.*
- *Supervise the maintenance of CAHS computer systems, and support IT Coordinator.*
- *Supervise the maintenance of the web site.*
- *Other duties and tasks as assigned.*

Responsible for maintaining good customer service at all levels of shelter contacts. The above statements are intended to describe the general nature and level of the work being performed by people assigned this classification. They are not to be construed as an exhaustive list of all job duties performed by the personnel so classified. This position is in FLSA category "Exempt." The Society has the right to revise this Position Description at any time. The Position Description is not a contract for employment and either the employee or the Society may terminate employment any time for any reason.

Fort Wayne Animal Care and Control

VOLUNTEER COORDINATOR
ANIMAL CARE & CONTROL

Working under the direction of the Director of Animal Care & Control, incumbent is responsible for the recruitment, programming, coordination, supervision, and training of volunteers for the shelter and community outreach programming.

DUTIES/ESSENTIAL FUNCTIONS:

- Recruit, supervise, and evaluate volunteers;
- Work with supervisors of the department to coordinate use of volunteers in appropriate areas of the agency and in outreach programming;
- Establish and maintain volunteer programming;
- Organize and conduct volunteer orientations;
- Responsible for volunteer training and oversight of volunteer training by staff members;
- Facilitate interaction between volunteers and full-time staff;
- Organize and conduct monthly "brown bag dinner" training opportunities for volunteers;
- Responsible for staffing volunteers to various tasks including but not limited to: on-site adoption programming, off-site adoption programming, animal rescue work, dog walkers and socializers, information and clerical desk work, cat room monitors and socializers, humane education programming, fund-raisers, special events, and the lost and found program;
- Establish ongoing liaisons within the community to facilitate the recruitment of volunteers;
- Responsible for recognizing, and when necessary, terminating the volunteer relationship of an individual who may not be appropriate for the program;
- Design, implement, and keep current volunteer applications, the screening process, and a volunteer handbook;
- Maintain database of volunteers inclusive of personal and contact information, skills, hours of desired volunteering, and hours donated;
- Design, research, and implement ongoing recognition, appreciation, and motivational programming for volunteers;
- Attend events as needed when volunteers are involved in order to ensure smooth operation;
- Create an annual or biannual newsletter for volunteers;
- Maintain valid Indiana driver's license.

MARGINAL FUNCTIONS:

- Perform various other duties as assigned.

continued…

MINIMUM REQUIREMENTS:

- Associate degree in a social science or liberal arts area with two years in volunteer supervisory capacity or five years experience in a volunteer coordinator's or similar position;
- Strong organizational skills with the ability to attract, maintain, train, supervise, encourage, and reward volunteers;
- The ability to learn and convey the concepts of governmental animal control, pet overpopulation, responsible pet ownership, animal care and handling, and euthanasia;
- Must have excellent written and verbal communication skills and be self-motivating.

DIFFICULTY OF WORK:

Incumbent works with generally accepted methods of operation but must use judgement in selecting pertinent guidelines and in adapting standard methods to ensure motivational, positive, safe, and rewarding experiences for volunteers. Incumbent must deal with intricate personnel/volunteer interactions as well as with volunteer relationships with the animals and the public. Incumbent works in the shelter and out in the community in hands-on activities with both animals and volunteers as well as in public speaking environments.

RESPONSIBILITY:

Incumbent is responsible for the activities of the volunteers and their interactions with the public, with staff, with the animals, and with one another. Incumbent is expected to make substantial contributions to structure, design, and maintenance of the entire volunteer program. Unusual problems or deviations from departmental guidelines may be discussed with the supervisor at the discretion of the incumbent.

PERSONAL WORK RELATIONSHIPS:

Incumbent has frequent daily contact with staff, volunteers, the general public, and social shelter animals to provide service, carry out tasks, and maintain coordination within the department.

SUPERVISION:

Incumbent supervises and trains volunteers at various times of work day and weekend.

LICENSE NEEDED: Valid Indiana driver's license

IMMEDIATE SUPERVISOR: Director of Animal Care & Control

HOURS: 9:00am to 6pm, will vary depending on need and hours of programming.

Involving Staff in Volunteer Management

In *Training Busy Staff to Succeed with Volunteers*, Betty Stallings points out that, in the past, too many organizations expected the volunteer coordinator to handle all aspects of interviewing, training, and supervising of volunteers. "It has now become obvious that successful volunteer programs involve both the commitment and competence of all staff within an organization," writes Stallings (1998, 13). To be effective, volunteer coordinators (with support from the executive leadership) must spend as much, if not more, time working with the staff who will be working with the volunteers. Coordinators need to train staff in how to manage volunteers. The program can't succeed without staff and the staff can't succeed without training.

You should first determine what staff members already know and what they need to learn to be comfortable working with volunteers. Once you identify what they need, you can develop appropriate training. To be receptive to training, staff must perceive it as valuable. Stallings (1998, 43) suggests, "Rather than inviting them to a workshop on interviewing volunteers, invite them to learn the skills in designing interview questions that will screen in the right volunteers."

Other than providing a simple overview about how the volunteer program works, many organizations give staff too little support for and training in working with volunteers. "The volunteer program can be meticulously structured and may pride itself on recruiting wonderful volunteers," says Stallings (1998, 37), "but if these volunteers work with staff who are neither committed nor competent in utilizing volunteers, the volunteer revolving door syndrome may occur. This often results in staff comments such as, 'See, volunteers are not reliable'—the death [knell] to a volunteer program."

Need help to train staff to work effectively with volunteers? See Resources for suggestions. Don't forget to check with your local community volunteer center to see if it offers training for staff in working with volunteers.

Tips for Supervising Volunteers

Shelter staff must do more than just work well with volunteers; many employees must supervise them well, too. The volunteer coordinator can't do everything alone. It's critical that volunteers are supervised properly to ensure consistent work and volunteer satisfaction. Volunteers need to receive appropriate and consistent feedback, including periodic evaluations of their performance. On the next page are some tips for supervising volunteers.

Table 6

Volunteers Stop Volunteering for an Organization Because:

Of demands on time	65 percent
No longer involved	32 percent
Of poor volunteer management practices:	
Not well managed	26 percent
Not good use of time	23 percent
Not good use of talents	18 percent
Tasks not clearly defined	16 percent
Not thanked	9 percent

A successful volunteer program requires strong management by the organization. Volunteers aren't going to continue coming back if they feel their time is being wasted or the organization isn't well-structured.

Source: UPS Foundation 1998.

■ **Treat volunteers as the professionals they are.** Never treat volunteers as second-class help. If you mistreat them, they will leave. They don't receive a paycheck as an incentive to stay as staff do.

■ **Expect a certain level of socializing with volunteers.** A little socializing among volunteers is fine as long as it doesn't disrupt their work or the staff. In fact, if volunteers make friends within the organization and feel connected, they'll probably stick around longer.

■ **Empower your volunteers to think for themselves and to be autonomous.** Offer guidance and support but try not to dictate how everything should be done. Volunteers can be very creative and may bring a new perspective that you haven't considered. Although volunteers should not be allowed to change procedures dramatically on their own, be open to their suggestions. As you become more comfortable with a volunteer, you can gradually give him or her more authority. Monitor the volunteer's progress and provide feedback, not only to ensure that everything is all right but also to make him or her feel like a valuable part of the team.

■ **Evaluate volunteers regularly.** Assess volunteers' performance based on their job descriptions. Tell volunteers how they're doing and get their feedback on their jobs and the overall volunteer program, too. Review the job description and make changes as necessary. Do not wait until the performance review to address a problem: talk to the volunteer immediately whenever a problem arises. In the evaluation, be sure to talk about more than just progress and problems: discuss long-range goals and offer praise for good work.

■ **Praise volunteers immediately for a job well done.** "Catch" volunteers doing the right thing and praise them for it. If they did a great job counseling an adopter, tell them so. Reinforce good behavior by noticing and acknowledging it. Doing so will build volunteer confidence and commitment to the program.

■ **Address problems with volunteers immediately.** It is uncomfortable to confront a volunteer about poor performance. You don't want to sound ungrateful for the volunteer's help, but letting problems slide helps the problem grow, not go away. Give honest feedback from the beginning. All new volunteers are "in training," which provides a good opportunity for open dialogue about performance. Correct the problem, not the volunteer. If you see someone making a mistake, pull the volunteer aside and talk to him or her about what went wrong. All volunteers need guidance.

What to Do When Problems Arise

From time to time, problems with volunteers are bound to occur. However, if you have taken the time to create a solid program, you will have fewer and easier problems to solve. Be sure to deal with volunteer problems right away. Here's how:

1. **Investigate.** Be sure to find out all you can about a problem before addressing it. Listen to the volunteer's side of the story and, if appropriate, talk to others who were directly involved.

2. **If the volunteer is at fault, talk to him or her directly.** Keep the discussion focused on the written job description and the shelter's policies and procedures. These provide an objective basis for talking to a volunteer about problems. If the volunteer is acting outside of his or her job responsibility or is not following the policies in place, you have grounds to confront the individual.

3. **Ask the volunteer to suggest a solution to the problem.** For example, if the individual consistently shows up late for his or her shift, ask the volunteer what he or she needs to arrive on time. Does the volunteer need to revise his or her schedule? Should the volunteer just leave home a little earlier? Let the individual know that it's important that volunteers show up when they're scheduled. Be clear that you count on the volunteer and that he or she needs to be reliable.

4. **Consider reassigning the volunteer.** It may turn out that a volunteer just isn't suited for the job he or she has been given. If the individual is a good volunteer, consider moving him or her to a different volunteer position. Be sure to train the volunteer for the new job.

5. **Document the problem, discussion, and proposed remedy.** For serious or repeat problems, consider having the volunteer sign the document and put a copy in his or her file.

6. **Allow a "problem volunteer" to leave gracefully.** Sometimes, when problems are addressed, a volunteer may choose simply to leave the position. This can be a blessing and save you the hassle of repeat problems.

Can You Dismiss a Volunteer?

As uncomfortable as it may be, dismissing a volunteer is sometimes appropriate—and may be absolutely critical to maintain a successful program. If you don't dismiss a volunteer when necessary, you undermine your program for both staff and other volunteers. However, if you have followed the advice provided in this manual, you will likely avoid having to dismiss many volunteers.

Whenever a volunteer is dismissed, think about what went wrong and what could have been done to prevent the situation. If the volunteer was a poor fit, maybe there's a flaw in the screening process. If the volunteer overstepped boundaries, perhaps he or she was not given a clear position description. Were training and supervision lacking? After dismissing a volunteer, carefully analyze whether some adjustments to the program need to be made.

It's not always easy to predict problem behavior, so it's important to have a clear dismissal policy in place before problems arise. Management should develop a clear dismissal policy when it develops its volunteer program—before a dismissal is necessary. Include a statement in the volunteer manual about termination so volunteers know that you reserve the right to remove a volunteer from his or her position at any time for any reason.

Sometimes dismissal doesn't solve the problem. A disgruntled volunteer may contact the media, local officials, or board of directors to air grievances. Devise a plan now to address this situation. The more structured your program, the more likely you will be to rebuff or rebut an attack by a former volunteer. Addressing each situation promptly and dismissing a problem volunteer will most likely save your program, not damage it. The other volunteers and staff members will appreciate it.

Here are the steps to take when dismissing a volunteer:

Step 1: Be sure you have all the facts. Investigate what happened and give the volunteer a chance to explain. Don't base your decision on hearsay.

Step 2: Consider all your options before dismissing the volunteer. Can this person be reassigned?

Step 3: Keep all discussions focused on the volunteer's actions and performance.

Step 4: Inform the volunteer privately and consider having a third person present as a witness. Explain clearly the reason for termination.

Step 5: Once the decision has been made, don't debate, counsel, or argue. You can allow the volunteer to speak or vent concerns, but be careful not to let the individual go on too long. If you have addressed the concerns with the volunteer's performance along the way (and documented everything for your files), he or she should not be surprised by being dismissed.

Step 6: Keep a written record for your files.

Step 7: Inform relevant staff and volunteers, including the volunteer's co-workers. Be careful about what information is shared. Provide only the basic facts and avoid gossip.

Chapter 11

Retaining and Motivating Volunteers

In a First Side Partners study of nonprofit managers (Lindberg and Dooley 2002), respondents were asked to indicate the reasons why their volunteers gave their time and talents. In almost every instance, respondents listed the following reasons:

- Volunteers were motivated by the mission of the organization or those being helped by the organization.
- They wanted to give back to the community.
- They had been personally touched by the organization.
- They felt they were needed and made a difference.

As the researchers point out,

> It is interesting to note that almost no one indicated that volunteers came because of a need to be recognized or because of the cachet attached to a particular institution. A couple of institutions said that people came because they had a beautiful place in which to work or because they thought a particular institution would be fun. However, it was clear from further questioning of the managers at these institutions that, unless people had other motivations besides those, retention would be an issue long-term. (21)

The UPS Foundation's study (1998) found that only 31 percent of respondents indicated they would be very likely to volunteer for an organization that thanks them and recognizes their efforts. Recognition is very important, but it's not what motivates most people to volunteer. A strong volunteer program—one that integrates volunteers into the operation, provides clear volunteer roles, and creates meaningful work—motivates volunteers and encourages retention.

Tips for Motivating Volunteers

- **Communicate, communicate, communicate!** If there is open communication with volunteers in the organization, the program will run much more smoothly and volunteers will truly feel a part of the team.

- **Keep volunteers informed.** Your volunteers need to be kept abreast of relevant changes in your organization—just like staff. Communicate through a volunteer newsletter, e-mail list, or periodic volunteer meetings.

- **Address volunteers by name.** This may seem difficult if your shelter has a lot of volunteers, but it's important. Require name tags if you need the reminder, but always call volunteers by their names.

- **Learn a little bit about them.** Try to stay connected with volunteers as much as possible. Send a birthday card, remember pets' names. Such personal touches go a long way toward helping volunteers feel included. Promote what volunteers are doing or what's happening in their lives. Did a volunteer adopt a dog? Put a notice (and picture) in your organization's newsletter. Did one of your volunteers recently get married? Announce it on the volunteer bulletin board to let others know. Create a community.

- **Help volunteers make friends.** A large component of volunteering is social. The more connected volunteers are to others in your organization, the longer they'll stay. Developing teams to work together on projects and providing a cheerful lounge or meeting room can enhance this social component.

- **Help them see the difference they make.** At the Champaign County (Illinois) Humane Society, the volunteer coordinator calls or e-mails a volunteer when an animal the volunteer is attached to is adopted. It provides the volunteer with one more chance to visit with the animal and say goodbye. The response has been great, and the volunteers feel more connected to the shelter and can see the great end result of their work.

- **Know what motivates them.** Why do people volunteer with your shelter? Every volunteer has different needs and motivations. Understanding what makes people passionate about their volunteer work can help you identify the proper way to thank them for their efforts.

- **Set high expectations.** Volunteers usually leave their assignments because they are underused, not because they are overworked. Help build their self-esteem by giving them meaningful and challenging assignments.

- **Invite volunteers to training events and workshops offered to paid staff.** You can handpick some of your best volunteers for advanced educational opportunities. Not only will the shelter gain better-trained volunteers, but the volunteers will feel honored by the opportunity as well. Post a calendar of upcoming training opportunities where volunteers can see it and sign up.

- **Involve volunteers in the decision-making process.** Considering developing a new program? Brainstorming ideas to improve community outreach? Ask a few volunteer representatives to attend your meetings. They are your ambassadors and may have some great ideas to contribute.

- **Offer volunteer promotions.** Once volunteers are doing well in their position and you're comfortable with their work, you can help them grow by offering new opportunities and more responsibility. Be sure to put your requirements for volunteer advancement in writing to ensure equal treatment and avoid discrimination. Keep in mind, however, that not every volunteer will want to take on more obligations. A volunteer may be happy serving as an office assistant for years and may not want a promotion. So make sure you know what your individual volunteers want and need to be happy.

- **Let them lead.** Volunteer leaders can help train new volunteers, oversee teams of volunteers, and develop new programs. This provides a rewarding experience for volunteer leaders and can free up staff time.

- **Offer advanced volunteer positions.** At the Humane Society at Lollypop Farm, volunteers are handpicked for the docent program, which trains volunteers to be tour guides for the shelter. Trained in all aspects of the operation, these high-level volunteers can answer any questions that arise during public tours of the facility.

- **Provide a few perks.** At Fort Wayne Animal Care and Control, the volunteer coordinator keeps a small refrigerator and snacks in her office. She finds out what the volunteers like to drink and makes sure she has their favorites on hand during their shift. When volunteers come by to get their snack, she can check in with them and see how things are going.

Recognizing the Work of Volunteers

- **Say thank you often and mean it!** Sometimes the simplest forms of recognition mean the most.

- **When recognizing a volunteer, be specific.** Recognize the volunteer for a particular job he or she did and specify how it helped the organization. Don't give empty praise. It needs to be tangible to be meaningful.

- **If your volunteers have done something exceptional, consider getting publicity for their work in the local media.** Public recognition can be a great motivator for your volunteers and provides positive coverage for your organization.

- **Feature the work of volunteers in your newsletter.** The Auckland (New Zealand) SPCA published a wonderful collage of photographs of volunteers working at the shelter.

- **Consider selecting a "Volunteer of the Month"** and highlight the accomplishments of a different volunteer each month.

- **Hold an annual banquet.** While a sincere thank you means more to many than any fancy award, volunteer picnics, informal recognition dinners, and simple awards can all become integral parts of a volunteer recognition effort. Some volunteers may not want a lavish appreciation event, believing that it's important for the organization's money to be spent on the animals, but you may be able to find local businesses to sponsor it. Local restaurants may be willing to donate gift certificates or cater food at your recognition ceremony.

- **Hold a staff-volunteer pizza party.** Inviting both staff and volunteers can serve as a great team builder.

- **Invite junior volunteers or foster families to an ice cream social.**

- **If you have a small store connected to your shelter, offer discounts or gift certificates to deserving volunteers.** Better yet, provide a discount as an ongoing benefit of simply being a volunteer!

- **Send anniversary cards and pins commemorating the number of years of volunteer service.**

- **Create a certificate of appreciation and specify the goals volunteers have helped the shelter accomplish over the last year.**

- **Hold your recognition events during national weeks devoted to volunteerism (see page 110 for a list).**

Ask Volunteers for Feedback

Volunteers want to be involved! Asking for their input can be very motivating. Design a questionnaire that invites feedback from volunteers about the strengths and weaknesses of your program so you can make improvements. Consider scheduling time to meet with representative volunteers individually and in small groups as a "think tank." This doubles as meaningful volunteer recognition while demonstrating the value of volunteer participation.

You can also provide a suggestion box for volunteers—and staff—to solicit anonymous feedback about what can be done to improve the volunteer program. To encourage participation, consider posting an open-ended question such as, Why do you really like volunteering here? or What do you wish we had to help you do your job here better?

Don't ask for feedback and then ignore it. Make a concerted effort to improve the program based on volunteer suggestions. Inform volunteers of these changes by posting them on the volunteer bulletin board or sending an e-mail thank you for the idea.

Monadnock Humane Society
Confidential Exit Interview—Volunteer

Name: _____

Primary Duties: _____

_____

Date of Separation: _____

1. What is your primary reason for leaving MHS?

    ❏ Volunteer experiences not what expected   ❏ Better volunteer experience

    ❏ Personality conflict   ❏ Home responsibilities

    ❏ Time constraints   ❏ Health

    ❏ Working conditions   ❏ Other

Please explain: _____

_____

_____

2. What did you think of:

	Poor	Fair	Average	Good	Excellent
Your co-volunteers	❏	❏	❏	❏	❏
MHS staff	❏	❏	❏	❏	❏
Your supervisor	❏	❏	❏	❏	❏
Your hours of service	❏	❏	❏	❏	❏
Your training	❏	❏	❏	❏	❏
Your volunteer experience	❏	❏	❏	❏	❏

3. What do you think about the facility's policies and how they are administered?

_____

_____

4. Do you feel that the work you did at MHS was important, and that you were a valuable part of this facility? Please explain your answer. _____

_____

_____

5. If you could change anything about MHS, what would it be and why would you change it? _____

_____

_____

_____

6. What do you think about the volunteer opportunities offered at the facility? Any suggestions for new opportunities or improvements? _____

_____

_____

7. How do you feel concerning your overall volunteer experience at the Monadnock Humane Society? _____

_____

_____

_____

8. Additional Comments:

Would you like any further information concerning alternative volunteer opportunities?
❏ Yes   ❏ No

Would you like to be called for future events?
❏ Yes   ❏ No

Conclusion

The UPS Foundation created the following chart so grant seekers can identify the strengths and weaknesses of the infrastructure supporting their organization's volunteer efforts. This is a great tool to help you chart your progress as you develop your volunteer program. So, go forth, plan well, have fun—**AND MAKE A DIFFERENCE IN THE LIVES OF ANIMALS!**

Elements of Volunteer Resources Management	Currently in place to some degree	Currently in place to a large degree	Not currently being done	Not applicable or not relevant
Written statement of philosophy related to volunteer involvement				
Orientation for new paid staff about why and how volunteers are involved in the organization's work				
Designated manager/leader for overseeing management of volunteers agency-wide				
Periodic needs assessment to determine how volunteers should be involved to address the mission				
Written position descriptions for volunteer roles				
Written policies and procedures for volunteer involvement				
Organizational budget reflects expenses related to volunteer involvement				
Periodic risk management assessment related to volunteer roles				
Liability insurance coverage for volunteers				
Specific strategies for ongoing volunteer recruitment				
Standardized screening and matching procedures for determining appropriate placement of volunteers				
Consistent general orientation for new volunteers				
Consistent training for new volunteers regarding specific duties and responsibilities				
Designated supervisors for all volunteer roles				
Periodic assessments of volunteer performance				
Periodic assessments of staff support for volunteers				
Consistent activities for recognizing volunteer contributions				
Consistent activities for recognizing staff support for volunteers				
Regular collection of information (numerical and anecdotal) regarding volunteer involvement				
Information related to volunteer involvement is shared with board members and other stakeholders at least twice annually				
Volunteer resources manager and fund development manager work closely together				
Volunteer resources manager is included in top-level planning				
Volunteer involvement is linked to organizational or program outcomes				

Chart reprinted from A Guide to Investing in Volunteer Resources Management: Improve Your Philanthropic Portfolio *with permission from the UPS Foundation,* www.community.ups.com.

Literature Cited

Ellis, S.J. 1996. *From the top down: The executive role in volunteer program success.* Philadelphia: Energize, Inc.

Ellis, S.J., and K.H. Noyes. 1990. *Proof positive: Developing significant volunteer recordkeeping systems.* Philadelphia: Energize, Inc.

Farmer, S.M., and D.B. Fedor. 2001. Changing the focus on volunteering: An investigation of volunteers' multiple contributions for a charitable organization. *Journal of Management* 27 (March–April): 191.

Herman, M., and P. Jackson. 2001. *No surprises: Harmonizing risk and reward in volunteer management.* Washington, D.C.: Nonprofit Risk Management Center.

Independent Sector. 2001. *Giving and volunteering in the United States.* Washington, D.C.: Independent Sector.

Lindberg, M.L., and M. Dooley. 2002. *Volunteerism, social capital and philanthropy in the not-for-profit sector: A research study.* First Side Partners, Consultants to Non-Profits. January. (*www.firstsidepartners.com*).

McCurley, S., and R. Lynch. 1996. *Volunteer management: Mobilizing all the resources of the community.* Darien, Ill.: Heritage Arts Publishing.

Peter D. Hart Research Associates. 2002. *The new face of retirement: An ongoing survey of American attitudes on aging.* Civic Ventures. August.

Safrit, R.D., and M. Merril. 2002. Management implications of contemporary trends in volunteerism in the United States and Canada. *The Journal of Volunteer Administration* 20 (2): 12–23.

Scheier, I.H. 1993. *Building staff/volunteer relations.* Philadelphia: Energize, Inc.

Stallings, B.B. 1998. *Training busy staff to succeed with volunteers: Building commitment and competence in staff/volunteer teams.* Pleasanton, Calif.: Building Better Skills.

UPS Foundation. 1998. *Managing volunteers: A report from United Parcel Service.* Published online at *www.community.ups.com/downloads/pdfs/1998_survey.pdf.*

The Urban Institute. 2004. *Volunteer management capacity in America's charities and congregations: A briefing report.* The Urban Institute. February. *www.urban.org/UploadedPDF/410963_Volunteer Managment.pdf.*

U.S. Department of Labor, Bureau of Labor Statistics. 2003. *Volunteering in the United States: 2003.* Online at *www.bls.gov/news.release/volun.nr0.htm.* Washington, D.C.

U.S. Department of Education, National Center for Education Statistics, FastResponse Survey System (FRSS). 1999. National student service— Learning and community service survey. FRSS 71. (*http://nces.ed.gov/quicktables/Detail.asp?Key=201*).

Vineyard, S. 2000. Retention of volunteers: A basic primer. *Grapevine* (September–October): 15.

Recommended Reading

Allison, M., and J. Kaye. 1997. *Strategic planning for nonprofit organizations: A practical guide and workbook*. New York: John Wiley and Sons.

American Humane Association (AHA). 1999. *Volunteer management: Operational guide for animal care and control agencies*. Englewood, Colo.: AHA.

Bryson, J.M. 1995. *Strategic planning for public and nonprofit organizations: A guide to strengthening and sustaining organizational achievement*. San Francisco: Jossey-Bass Publishers.

Ellis, S. 1996. *The volunteer recruitment (and membership development) book*. Philadelphia: Energize, Inc.

Ellis, S.J., A. Weisbord, and K.H. Noyes. 1991. *Children as volunteers: Preparing for community service*. Philadelphia: Energize, Inc.

Graff, L.L. 1997. *By definition: Policies for volunteer programs*. Dundas, Ontario, Canada: Graff and Associates.

The Humane Society of the United States. 2002. *How to do almost anything in the shelter*. (www.AnimalSheltering.org).

Lee, J.F., with J.M. Catagnus. 1999. *What we learned (the hard way) about supervising volunteers: An action guide for making your job easier*. Philadelphia: Energize, Inc.

McCurley, S., and S. Vineyard. 1998. *Handling problem volunteers*. Darien: Ill.: Heritage Arts Publishing.

Minnesota Office of Citizenship and Volunteer Services. 1998. *How to control liability and risk in volunteer programs*. St. Paul: Minnesota Office of Citizenship and Volunteer Services.

Stallings, B. 1998. *Training busy staff to succeed with volunteers: Building commitment and competence in staff/volunteer teams*. Pleasanton, Calif.: Building Better Skills.

Vineyard, S., and S. McCurley. 2001. *Best practices for volunteer programs: Best ideas from best programs*. Darien, Ill.: Heritage Arts Publishing.

Internet Resources

Animal Sheltering Online
www.AnimalSheltering.org
Web site for *Animal Sheltering* magazine and
other resources from The HSUS

BoardSource
www.boardsource.org
Web site devoted to nonprofit board development

Charity Village
www.charityvillage.com
Canada's supersite for the nonprofit
sector; includes volunteer program
survey and assessment tools

CyberVPM
www.avaintl.org/network/cybervpm.html
Listserv for professional managers
of volunteer programs

e-Volunteerism
http://e-volunteerism.com
Online journal about volunteerism

Humane Society University
www.HumaneSocietyU.org
Training and professional development
for the field of animal care and control

The Independent Sector
www.independentsector.org
Contains a wealth of research and
resources on nonprofit management

Internet Nonprofit Center
www.nonprofits.org
Frequently asked questions about nonprofits
and bibliography of books on volunteerism

**Management Assistance Program
for Nonprofits**
www.mapfornonprofits.org
Provides links to information about
managing volunteer programs

Nonprofit Genie
www.genie.org
Resources for the nonprofit community

Points of Light
www.pointsoflight.org/centers/find_center.cfm
Provides a list of volunteer centers nationwide

**Shelter Volunteer Management
Discussion Group**
www.AnimalSheltering.org/volunteermanagement
E-mail group for managers of volunteers who
work with animal shelters, breed placement
groups, and other animal care organizations

USA Freedom Corps
www.usafreedomcorps.gov
A network of resources on volunteerism

Volunteer Today
www.volunteertoday.com
Electronic gazette for volunteerism

Magazines and Newsletters

***Animal Sheltering* magazine**
(bimonthly)
$12 one year subscription,
$18 two years subscription
The Humane Society of the United States
2100 L Street, NW
Washington, DC 20037-1598
202-452-1100; Fax: 301-258-3081
www.AnimalSheltering.org

Charity Channel's *Volunteer Management Review*
(e-mail newsletter)
Sign up for free online at
http://charitychannel.com/enewsletters/vmr/index.asp

Energize Update
(e-mail newsletter)
Sign up for free online at
www.energizeinc.com

Grapevine
(Volunteer Management Newsletter)
$25 annual subscription (bimonthly)
Volunteer Marketplace
Points of Light Foundation
800-272-8306
PDF file downloadable at
www.energizeinc.com

Volunteer Management Report
$119 annual subscription
Stevenson, Inc.
P.O. Box 4528
Sioux City, IA 51104
712-239-3010; Fax: 712-239-2166
www.stevensoninc.com

Volunteer Management-Related Organizations

American Society for Directors of Volunteer Services
One North Franklin
27th Floor
Chicago, IL 60606
312-422-3939; Fax: 312-422-4575
www.asdvs.org

Association for Research on Nonprofit Organizations and Voluntary Action
550 West North Street
Suite 301
Indianapolis, IN 46202
317-684-2120; Fax: 317-684-2128
www.arnova.org

Association for Volunteer Administration
P.O. Box 32092
Richmond, VA 23294
804-672-3353; Fax: 804-672-3368
www.avaintl.org

BoardSource
1828 L Street, NW
Suite 900
Washington, DC 20036-5114
202-452-6262 or 800-883-6262;
Fax 202-452-6299
www.boardsource.org

Energize, Inc.
5450 Wissahickon Avenue
Philadelphia, PA 19144
215-438-8342; Fax: 215-438-0434
www.energizeinc.com

Nonprofit Risk Management Center
1130 Seventeenth Street, NW
Suite 210
Washington, DC 20036
202-785-3891; Fax: 202-296-0349
www.nonprofitrisk.org

The Points of Light Foundation
1400 I Street, NW
Suite 800
Washington, DC 20005
202-729-8000; Fax: 202-729-8100
www.pointsoflight.org

Special Days and Weeks Devoted to Volunteerism

These are opportunities for your organization to recognize the work of current volunteers or to recruit new ones.

Random Acts of Kindness Week
February 14–20, 2005
February 13–19, 2006
February 12–18, 2007
Sponsor: Random Acts of Kindness Foundation
1801 Broadway Street, Suite 250
Denver, CO 80202
800-660-2811; *www.actsofkindness.org*

National Volunteer Week
April 17–24, 2005
April 23–29, 2006
April 15–21, 2007
Sponsor: Points of Light Foundation
1400 I Street, NW, Suite 800
Washington, DC 20005
800-VOLUNTEER; *www.pointsoflight.org/NVW*

National Youth Service Day
April 15–17, 2005
Sponsor: Youth Service America
1101 Fifteenth Street, NW, Suite 200
Washington, DC 20005
202-296-2992; *www.ysa.org/nysd*

Join Hands Day
May 7, 2005
May 6, 2006
May 5, 2007
Sponsor: National Fraternal
Congress of America
1240 Iroquois Avenue, Suite 301
Naperville, IL 60563
877-OUR-1DAY; *www.joinhandsday.org*

Make A Difference Day
(held the fourth Saturday every October)
October 22, 2005
October 28, 2006
October 27, 2007
Sponsor: *USA Weekend Magazine*
and Points of Light Foundation
diffday@usaweekend.com
www.makeadifferenceday.com

National Animal Shelter Appreciation Week
(held the first full week of November each year, beginning on Sunday)
November 6–12, 2005
November 5–11, 2006
November 4–10, 2007
Sponsor: The Humane Society
of the United States
2100 L Street, NW
Washington, DC 20037
202-452-1100; *www.AnimalSheltering.org*

National Family Volunteer Day
November 19, 2005
Sponsor: Points of Light Foundation and
the Alliance for Children and Families
1400 I Street, NW, Suite 800
Washington, DC 20005
1-800-VOLUNTEER; *www.pointsoflight.org*

Organizations Offering Volunteer Recognition Products

Harrison Promotions, Inc.
7926 Queen Street
Wyndmoor, PA 19038
800-929-2271
www.harrisonpromotions.com

Philanthropic GIFT
12501 Old Columbia Pike
Silver Spring, MD 20904
800-622-1662
www.philanthropicgift.com

The Thanks Company
114 Cone Street
P.O. Box 220
Cherryville NC 28021-0220
888-875-0903
www.thankscompany.com

VolunteerGifts.com
1700 N. Dixie Highway
Suite 103
Boca Raton, FL 33432
800-293-0032
www.VolunteerGifts.com

HSUS Volunteer Management Survey

HUMANE SOCIETY
UNIVERSITY

VOLUNTEER SURVEY

Please complete the form below, print it out by clicking the Print Now button, and mail it to:
Humane Society University
700 Professional Drive
Gaithersburg, MD 20879

GENERAL INFORMATION ABOUT YOUR ORGANIZATION _____

Your Name _____

Your Title _____

Organization _____

Address (Line 1)_____

Address (Line 2)_____

City _____ State _____ Zip/Postal Code _____

Phone Number _____ Your E-mail Address _____

How many animals does your organization handle each year? _____

Our organization is a . . . (select one)

❏ Municipal animal control agency

❏ Private humane organization

❏ Private humane organization with contract
to provide animal control services

❏ Private humane organization with housing
contract for an animal control agency

What kind of insurance coverage do you have for volunteers?

❏ Volunteers are covered under
  our organization's insurance

❏ We require volunteers to have their own insurance

❏ Other (please indicate): _____

❏ I don't know

Which of the following tools do you use in your volunteer program?

(Please indicate all that apply.)

❏ Job Descriptions

❏ Orientations/Interviews

❏ Formal Training

❏ Applications

❏ Liability Waiver

❏ Volunteer Performance Reviews

❏ Recognition Events

❏ Volunteer Manual

❏ Volunteer Contract

❏ Volunteer Schedule

❏ Other (please indicate): _____

STAFF INVOLVEMENT _____

How much staff time is currently devoted to specifically managing volunteers?

❏ We have a full-time position dedicated
  only to managing volunteers

❏ We have a full-time position that manages
  volunteers as well as many other things

❏ We have a part-time position
  that manages volunteers

❏ Other (please indicate): _____

What is the job title of the person who manages the volunteer program? _____

_____

Staff feels volunteers are . . .

❏ Very helpful

❏ Somewhat helpful

❏ No opinion

❏ OK, but not that helpful

❏ Disruptive to daily work

TYPES OF VOLUNTEERS AND HOURS WORKED _____

How many volunteers do you currently have?

_____ Active (volunteers on a regular basis
of at least 5 hours per month)

_____ Inactive (volunteers infrequently)

If possible, please break down your ACTIVE volunteers
(an active volunteer contributes at least 5 hours per month) according to the following

* *(Please include only those board members who volunteer hands-on with day-to-day activities—not official board activities)*

	Number Who Actively Volunteer	Total Combined Hours Volunteered per Month
Board Members*		
Retired Community Members		
Adult Community Members		
Teens 16–18		
Kids under 16		

**What length of time do you ask volunteers to commit to volunteering
for your organization** (for example, a minimum commitment of 3 months)? _____

**Approximately how many hours per week do volunteers work
during the following time periods?**

	Weekdays	Weekends
Morning (7 a.m. to Noon)		
Afternoon (Noon to 5 p.m.)		
Evening (5 p.m. or later)		

KIDS AND TEEN VOLUNTEERS_____

**Please explain the volunteer activities kids may perform in your
organization, noting age restrictions** (Please check all that apply):

❏ We do not accept kids under the age of _____
as volunteers in the organization

❏ Kids under the age of _____ are not permitted
to have hands-on interaction with animals

❏ Parents must supervise their kids during their kids'
volunteer time if the kids are under the age of _____

❏ Other (please indicate): _____

How does your organization feel about kids as volunteers?

❏ Works great; the kids are helpful
   and we like having them

❏ Somewhat helpful

❏ No opinion

❏ OK, but not that helpful

❏ The kids are too much work
   and not worth the hassle

❏ Other (please indicate): _____

BOARD MEMBER VOLUNTEERS _____

**How well does the board member hands-on involvement
in day-to-day activities work for the organization**
(if any of your board members participate this way)**?**

❏ Works great; the board members are helpful and we
   like having them involved in day-to-day activities

❏ Somewhat helpful

❏ No opinion

❏ OK, but not that helpful

❏ The board members cause problems
   by interfering in day-to-day activities

❏ Board members are not permitted to
   be involved in day-to-day activities

❏ Other (please indicate): _____

VOLUNTEER RECRUITMENT _____
How do you advertise for volunteers?
(Please indicate all that apply.)

❏ Newsletter

❏ web site

❏ Ads in community newspapers,
   on bulletin boards, etc.

❏ We don't advertise our volunteer program

❏ Other (please indicate): _____

What times of day is volunteer help lacking?

❏ Weekdays during the day

❏ Weekday evenings

❏ Weekends

❏ Other (please indicate): _____

VOLUNTEER ASSIGNMENTS

Please check the jobs your volunteers currently do for you.
(Please indicate all that apply.)

- ❏ Adoption Counseling
- ❏ Clerical (Data Entry, Filing, Typing)
- ❏ Customer Service (Receptionist)
- ❏ Foster Care
- ❏ Socialize/Walk Dogs
- ❏ Socialize Cats
- ❏ Small Mammal Companionship
- ❏ Dog Training
- ❏ Humane Education
- ❏ Kennel and Cage Cleaning
- ❏ Veterinary Assistance
- ❏ Gift Shop Management
- ❏ Fund Raising
- ❏ Special Events
- ❏ Animal Assisted Therapy
- ❏ Grooming
- ❏ Other (please indicate): _____

In which volunteer assignments did you have the most turnover in the last year and why? _____

_____

Which volunteer assignments are the most popular with volunteers and why? _____

_____

Please list three areas of your overall operation that require the most help:

1. _____
2. _____
3. _____

Have you tried using volunteers in those areas?

- ❏ Yes
- ❏ No

Did it work well? Why or why not? _____

_____

Can you identify what you were able to do more of in the past year than last because of the extra help from volunteers? _____

_____

_____

VOLUNTEER TRAINING _____

How do you train your volunteers?

Please choose the method below that most applies.

❏ We have a formal volunteer training program run by paid staff using written training materials such as a manual

❏ We do not have a formal volunteer training program, but volunteers shadow the staff and learn the ropes that way

❏ We do not have a formal staff-run volunteer training program, but current volunteers train new volunteers

❏ We don't have a formal volunteer training program

❏ Other (please indicate): _____

Please indicate which methods of training you provide to your STAFF on how to manage volunteers:

❏ In-house training sessions

❏ We send them to training off-site

❏ They learn on the job

❏ We do not provide training

❏ Other (please indicate): _____

Please indicate what written procedures you provide for your STAFF on day-to-day activities:

❏ We have written standard operating procedures available for all staff

❏ We have signs posted throughout the facility with instructions on how to perform tasks

❏ We do not have any written procedures

❏ Other (please indicate): _____

VOLUNTEER RECOGNITION _____

Please indicate the ways you recognize the work of your VOLUNTEERS:

❏ We say Thank You

❏ We hold a special recognition event

❏ We currently don't recognize our volunteers

❏ Other (please indicate): _____

Please indicate the ways you recognize the work of your STAFF:

❏ Raises and promotions

❏ We say Thank You

❏ We hold a special recognition event

❏ Other (please indicate): _____

VOLUNTEER RETENTION

Approximately what percentage of the people who apply to be a volunteer or attend an orientation actually come back and volunteer with your organization? _____ percent

How long does a volunteer typically stay with your organization?

- ❏ Less than 1 month
- ❏ 1–3 months
- ❏ 3–6 months
- ❏ 6 months–1 year
- ❏ More than 1 year
- ❏ I don't know

What are the three major reasons that volunteers give for stopping their volunteering?

1. _____
2. _____
3. _____

- ❏ I don't know. We don't gather such information.

Which group of volunteers stays on as volunteers the longest?

- ❏ Board members
- ❏ Retirees
- ❏ Adults
- ❏ Teens 16–18
- ❏ Kids under 16

Which group of volunteers has the most turnover?

- ❏ Board members
- ❏ Retirees
- ❏ Adults
- ❏ Teens 16–18
- ❏ Kids under 16

If you survey your volunteers, what are the reasons they give for staying? _____

_____

If you do NOT survey your volunteers, why do you think they stay? _____

_____

_____

Do you actively seek feedback from volunteers about their volunteer experience with your organization?

- ❏ Yes
- ❏ No

Have you fired a volunteer?

       ❑ Yes

       ❑ No

Why or why not? If yes, please explain the circumstances of one example. _____

_____

_____

CONCLUSION _____

What is currently working the best with your current volunteer program? _____

_____

_____

Where are you having the greatest difficulty with volunteers? _____

_____

_____

_____

**Do you keep any other statistics on your volunteer program
that you would be willing to share with us at a later time?**

       ❑ Yes

       ❑ No

Do you have any other thoughts or comments you would like to share?

If so, please use the space provided below. Also, feel free to suggest additional
questions that we might ask in future questionnaires.